IN THE ABSENCE
OF ORDERS

IN THE ABSENCE OF ORDERS

For we walk by faith, not by sight.
—2 Corinthians 5:7

KEVIN V. HOYER

iUniverse, Inc.
New York Lincoln Shanghai

IN THE ABSENCE OF ORDERS

For we walk by faith, not by sight. -2 Corinthians 5:7

iUniverse books may be ordered through booksellers or by contacting:

iUniverse
2021 Pine Lake Road, Suite 100
Lincoln, NE 68512
www.iuniverse.com
1-800-Authors (1-800-288-4677)

ISBN: 978-0-595-45313-9 (pbk)
ISBN: 978-0-595-89626-4 (ebk)

Printed in the United States of America

"Sometimes we feel as though we are navigating through this life not knowing what to do next or which way to go. Yet, if we really analyzed our situation and looked in the right direction in the right way, we would see that God is moving mountains on our behalf and clearly directing our steps."

For we walk by faith, not by sight.

—2 Corinthians 5:7

Now faith is the substance of things hoped for, the evidence of things not seen.

—Hebrews 11:1

CONTENTS

Introduction

Now faith is the substance of things hoped for, the evidence of things not seen.

—Hebrews 11:1

In this book we are going to explore the possibilities of faith. We will purposely bypass human reasoning, rational and wisdom, because human wisdom is an abomination to God! "For the wisdom of this world is folly with God. For it is written, 'He catches the wise in their craftiness,' and again, 'The Lord knows the thoughts of the wise, that they are futile'" (1 Cor. 3:19-20 ESV).

We will examine triumphant faith that surpasses the temporalness of this life. A faith that goes way beyond the obstacles to the possibilities and promises God has given us in His Word. A faith that transcends what is felt, seen, and heard by looking to the perfect one, Jesus, and the truth of His Word. There is absolutely nothing God won't do for those who love and obey Him and look to Him for all their needs.

We will look at the hindrances in our own lives as well as personal examples in the Bible of disobedience and unbelief that hindered faith. We will also look at numerous examples of triumphant faith and how God moved on their behalf. Throughout this book we will clearly show what faith is and what kind of faith God loves and reacts to. In the course of this book, my hope is that we will be stirred to seek Jesus Christ more and allow Him to produce a deeper obedient faith within our lives. The ultimate byproduct of this book is to have more stability, growth, and obedience in our walk with the Lord.

For we walk by faith, not by sight.

—2 Corinthians 5:7

The Word of God tells us that we are to "walk by faith" and not "by sight" (2 Cor. 5:7). But if most of us were to sincerely and honestly evaluate our faith, our walk would most likely look like we were "walking by sight" more than "walking by faith." When I look back and analyze my faith over the past few years, especially the trials I went through and how God worked them out, if I knew then what I know now, I would not have wasted so much time in unbelief, worry, and anxiety. Why? God was utterly faithful and worked every situation out perfectly according to His will. Not according to how I thought it would work out—dreaming, wishing, and dwelling too much on it—but worked it out perfectly His way, and in His time.

We can believe that God's Word is true and that He is utterly faithful, and yet be so driven and moved more by what we feel, see, and hear other people tell us, than to trust in God's Word, which is infallible. Or get upset when things don't work out the way we wanted, even though we believe that God is working everything out for our good and His Glory. Or get upset when we get stuck in a certain situation, even though we believe what the Word of God tells us: that everything happens in our lives, both good and bad for a purpose. "And we know that all things work together for good to them that love God, to them who are the called according to his purpose" (Rom. 8:28).

How we trust and yield our circumstances to God during those trials will determine the benefit and the outcome that we will receive from it. Our faith, attitude, and trust in God through our trials will determine if we grow spiritually and come out grateful and joyous towards God or the opposite: bitter and full of self-pity. Some people might even get angry with God because they want God to bless their worldly (security, ease) and materialistic wants, even though it is hindering their relationship with the Lord. But because God loves them, He will not allow that to happen. God loves us and desires above everything a relationship with us, and that is why He wants us to build faith and trust in Him no matter what is going on internally or externally. He does not want anything to hinder our relationship with Him.

Some Observations on Faith

1. We can trust the Word of God no matter what.

2. God loves us and has our best interests at heart.

3. What we see, feel, hear, and perceive is not always how it is.

4. We cannot use the world's standards (i.e., materialism, people's admiration and support, popularity, success, position) as a measure to determine if God is working in our lives or as a standard for measuring a ministry's success.

5. What we think we need is not always what we really need.

6. God desires to build faith and trust in our lives to do His will and to glorify Him.

7. The more we put our faith and trust in God and do His will, the more fruitful, joyful, and fulfilled our lives will be.

8. The opposite of faith is fear.

9. God determines the outcome of our situation, not man.

10. Our current condition and circumstances will not determine how our future will be.

11. It is never too late to change or start something new.

12. True faith in Christ produces obedience to His Word.

13. Obedient faith produces sanctified lives.

14. Without faith, it impossible to please God!

But without faith it is impossible to please him: for he that cometh to God must believe that he is, and that he is a rewarder of them that diligently seek him.

—Hebrews 11:6

The more we seek Jesus Christ, the more of His presence and power we will receive in our lives. What kind of power? We will have the power to obey God's Word, to separate from sin, as well as to overcome and resist temptation. The more filled we are with Jesus' life, the more we will believe and trust that what He said is true. In turn, we will better understand how He directs and speaks to us through His Word. The more we seek God and know His Word, the less we will allow the world's false philosophies, ideologies, fears, and cares to distract us and choke out the truth (Mark 4:19). If we are not immersing ourselves in the truth, then we easily succumb to the lies of this world because of the unbelief in our hearts.

The more truth we embrace, the more conviction of the Holy Spirit we will receive. This conviction is good because it shows us how unlike Christ we are, which is a great thing because it causes us to want God to change those areas that He has illuminated. He illuminates the sin in our lives so we can see it and give it to Him to change. This in turn produces a deeper faith, obedience, and holiness. In reality, true happiness, fulfillment, and joy comes from the Lord—not from people or things. It comes when we are in right standing with Him. When we are not in right standing with God, our lives become very superficial and are filled with inner turmoil and bondage.

If we totally put our faith and trust in God in every situation of our lives—in the good times as well as the bad—our lives would be filled with more joy and peace and be free from the day-to-day anxiety and stress of life. Why? We would be putting our faith and trust in God's character and His complete sovereignty in every situation of our lives. We would believe every one of His promises that He has promised us and trust that His words would come to pass. This in turn would bring us more joy and peace in our daily lives. "He who deals wisely and heeds [God's] word and counsel shall find good, and whoever leans on, trusts in, and is confident in the Lord—happy, blessed, and fortunate is he" (Prov. 16:20 AMP).

Nothing pleases God more than obedient faith. We need faith to please God. Obedient faith puts our trust in God and what He has clearly laid out for us in His Word. A clear sign we have faith in the Lord is when we believe what He has said and act on what He has told us—we obey Him! Faith pleases God because none of us have come to Him in our own strength. "No one is able to come to Me unless the Father Who sent Me attracts and draws him and gives him the desire to come to Me" (John 6:44 AMP). God the Father shows His love toward us by revealing Jesus Christ to us and by showing our need for Him. Through the conviction of the Holy Spirit, He shows us our sin and the need to repent. In turn, we respond to God by obeying Him and repenting (forsaking and turning) from our sinful lives to receive forgiveness. Then we turn our lives over to Jesus Christ to be totally transformed.

God has made a way for us to have forgiveness and eternal life and is continually drawing us, but we cannot receive salvation or any other thing from the Lord without responding to Him by faith—for He designed it that way. He has given us a personal responsibility to respond to Him by faith and obey Him. The more we draw closer to Him in the Word and in prayer, the more of God's truth will be revealed to us. As we respond to the truth and believe and obey it, the more we draw closer to Jesus Christ. The more we draw closer to Jesus Christ, the more of God's truth (Word) will be revealed to us and the easier it will be to obey (Matt. 13:12). Why will it be easier to obey? Because we are allowing the Holy Spirit to transform our lives, and in that transformation we have to get rid of those things that would hinder our growth. And as we draw closer to Jesus Christ, He empowers us by the Holy Spirit to have the ability to repent and separate from the sin and the obstacles that would hinder our obedience to Him. "So faith comes from hearing, and hearing through the word of Christ" (Rom. 10:17 ESV).

It is impossible to profess to have faith in Jesus Christ and live a life in complete rebellion and disobedience towards His commands. That is not called faith—that is called rejecting and resisting. We either live a life of faith in Christ that leads to eternal life or we spend our life rejecting and resisting the Holy Spirit's drawing. A life spent rejecting and resisting the Holy Spirit's draw to Jesus Christ for salvation leads to eternity in hell.

Genuine faith is an ongoing activity throughout our lives of putting faith and trust in Jesus Christ. When we put faith in something, it means that we allow it to do what it says it is supposed to do. Take the example of an elevator, we get in, push a few buttons, and have faith that it will take us to the floor we need to go to. Faith in Christ means that we put our trust in Him and allow Him to lead us. As we seek Him and read His Word, the Holy Spirit illuminates the Word and reveals who Jesus is and how we are to live. We in turn respond in agreement with the Holy Spirit and desire Him to change our hearts. We obey Him in whatever He wants us to accomplish for Him as well as whatever He wants us to change or to give up. He gives us the discernment and the power to guard against those things that would hinder our faith.

> *Looking unto Jesus the author and finisher of our faith; who for the joy that was set before him endured the cross, despising the shame, and is set down at the right hand of the throne of God.*
>
> —Hebrews 12:2

Jesus is the author and finisher of our faith. We need to look to Him and follow His example. He has given every "born again" believer a new life that He purchased with His own blood. Jesus did not succumb to the pressure to give up because of the pain and humiliation He was feeling. No, He didn't! Because Hebrews 12 states that "for the joy that was set before him [he] endured the cross." What was the joy? That He would redeem us by paying our penalty for sin. Through Him we would have the power to overcome sin and temptation (Rom. 6:14). Of the utmost importance is that we will be "born again." We are adopted into His family and will live eternally with Him.

Knowing all that Jesus has done for us, it would be utterly foolish and futile to seek and trust in anything other than Him. If we truly trusted God and allowed Him to work in our lives and believe what He has told us in His Word, we would naturally produce more genuine fruit. We would also have less worry, anxieties, and fears, which in turn would give us more peace, joy, energy, and direction. If we were to look closely into our lives, we would see that most of our fears and worries are unfounded and our anxieties and stress are self-imposed. God desires for us not to be bogged down with self-imposed burdens and unfounded fears, but to have the freedom to serve Him with joy.

> *Thou wilt shew me the path of life: in thy presence is fullness of joy; at thy right hand there are pleasures for evermore.*
>
> —Psalm 16:11

May His kingdom come!

Kevin V. Hoyer

CHAPTER 1

▼

IN THE OLIVE PRESS

And he came out and went, as was his custom, to the Mount of Olives, and the disciples followed him. And when he came to the place, he said to them, "Pray that you may not enter into temptation." And he withdrew from them about a stone's throw, and knelt down and prayed, saying, "Father, if you are willing, remove this cup from me. Nevertheless, not my will, but yours, be done." And there appeared to him an angel from heaven, strengthening him. And being in an agony he prayed more earnestly; and his sweat became like great drops of blood falling down to the ground. And when he rose from prayer, he came to the disciples and found them sleeping for sorrow, and he said to them, "Why are you sleeping? Rise and pray that you enter not into temptation."

—Luke 22:39-46 (ESV)

Jesus went up with His disciples to the Garden of Gethsemane on the Mount of Olives to pray. In Matthew 26:38, Jesus says, "My soul is exceeding sorrowful, even unto death: tarry ye hear, and watch with me." On this night, Jesus was in agony and inner turmoil as He anticipated the great personal sufferings He was about to face. This night was the last night Jesus would be alone with His disciples before being arrested. It would also be the last night Jesus would have alone to pray to the Father.

He went to the garden to pray to the Father because He was in deep agony knowing and thinking about what was about to happen. This night, one of His disciples would betray Him (Judas) and the rest would forsake Him. He was going to be arrested, falsely accused, physically abused, lied about, misunderstood, spit on, beaten, mocked, chastised, and crucified (nailed to a cross). During Jesus' upcoming trial, even His disciples were going to deny Him.

Most of Jesus' agony was probably due to the fact that He was going to take upon Himself the sin of the world. This would cause Him to be temporarily separated from the Father and experience God's wrath and punishment against sin. Sin was something that Jesus had never experienced, for He lived a sinless life making Him the perfect sacrifice. But now He was going to bear the sins of mankind. "For he hath made him to be sin for us, who knew no sin; that we might be made the righteousness of God in him" (2 Cor. 5:21). He was also going to experience God's wrath and punishment against sin for us. Jesus hated sin, because of the separation, destruction, and bondage it brought—that is why He came to save us from our sins (John 1:29).

Throughout Jesus' pre-earthly and earthly life, He had never experienced separation from the Father. He had always had uninterrupted communion with the Father even before the world began (John 17:5). He was also totally dependent on and obedient to the Father in every area of His life. Now He would have to experience this temporary separation from the Father *and* God's punishment for sin, because nothing that is unholy (sinful) can stand in God's presence. So taking on the sin of the world would cause Jesus to be separated from God the Father.

> *I have glorified You down here on the earth by completing the work that You gave Me to do.*
>
> —John 17:4 (AMP)

Jesus knew He had come to Earth to be a man, like the people He had created, in order to fulfill all of God's righteous requirements for the perfect sacrifice for them. During His time on Earth, He was fulfilling God's law by obeying the law both outwardly and inwardly. Jesus' earthly life fulfilled all the prophecies concerning Him, "which were written in the law of Moses, and in the prophets, and in the psalms, concerning me" (Luke 24:44). Now the last part of all the prophecies and the reason He was sent to the earth was ahead of Him—this great trial of affliction of being crucified on the cross. He must have felt very alone at this point, because even His disciples seemed oblivious to what was going to happen this night.

When Jesus got to the place in the garden where He wanted to pray, He told His disciples "Pray that you may not enter into temptation" (Luke 22:40 ESV). Jesus wanted His disciples to watch and to pray so that the night's events would not take them by surprise and overwhelm them, even though He had warned them about what was going to happen. Then Jesus went a short distance from His disciples to pray: "Father, if thou be willing, remove this cup from me: nevertheless not my will, but thine, be done" (Luke 22:42). Jesus prayed that "this cup" (this trial) would be removed from Him. He was in agony thinking about and anticipating the physical and spiritual torture that he was about to face and the reality and anticipation that the people He came to save would reject and crucify Him. The act of taking on himself the sin of the world would cause Him to be rejected by God and suffer God's wrath and punishment for sin. He was in such inner turmoil and agony that Luke 22:44 says, "And being in an agony he prayed more earnestly: and his sweat was as it were great drops of blood falling down to the ground."

Jesus was praying so hard that His sweat was like great drops of blood as He battled His fleshly desires to do things His own way instead of submitting to God's will. Yet even though Jesus was in great physical and spiritual agony, He did not succumb to His desires and seek personal comfort, as many of us would have done. No, He said, "nevertheless not my will, but thine, be done." He came to fulfill God's will and all that was written about Him (the Messiah). So instead of yielding to His own fleshly desires, and trying to get out of the whole situation, He submitted himself to God's will.

Immediately after Jesus submitted to God's will, God sent an angel to strengthen Him (Luke 22:43). Just like any trial we are about to face, if we submit ourselves to God's will He will pour out His grace and empower us to go through it. No matter our situation, if we submit to God's will the ultimate outcome will bear good fruit. That is exactly what Jesus did, because it was His Father's will for Him to die for the sins of the people. It was what He was sent to do. Jesus looked past His current situation with its spiritual and physical agony and saw what the outcome of His obedience would be—and it brought Him joy.

> *Looking unto Jesus the author and finisher of our faith; who for the joy that was set before him endured the cross, despising the shame, and is set down at the right hand of the throne of God.*
>
> —Hebrews 12:2

In the garden that night, Jesus persevered in obedience to the Father's will and did not succumb to the temptation to avoid the suffering. In fact He looked past the cross and saw the joy that His obedience would bring into the world. The joy He would feel at accomplishing all that the Father had given Him to do. The joy that He would give to His people by forgiving their sins and giving them His righteousness, so that they could be brought into a right standing with God the Father. The unending joy that He would experience in heaven with those who love Him for all of eternity. All the suffering was worth it to Jesus, in order that He could secure salvation for those who love Him.

We need to look to Jesus' obedient life as our example: "the author and finisher of our faith." Jesus persevered despite the fact that He could have stopped it at any time! He was God manifested in the flesh (1 Tim. 3:16). Yet, He came to fulfill the Father's will and complete the work He was sent to do: "I have glorified thee on the earth: I have finished the work which thou gavest me to do" (John 17:4). No matter how unbearable or impossible things get in our lives, staying firm in our faith and obedience to God's Word will bring about God's purpose—both in the situation and in our lives.

Looking and focusing on our impossible situations will cause bitterness and produce hopelessness. We will start to feel self-pity and blame others or ourselves, or even get mad at God for allowing this to happen. It's true that we, or others, can get ourselves into a lot of trouble and heartache, but focusing on our troubles will not bring us out of the situation with a good outcome. Only by submitting wholeheartedly to God's will, will good be produced out of the situation. It means that we need to lean on and diligently seek God in prayer until the situation is resolved. We need to resist the temptation to give up or give in and sin against God by disobeying Him. We need to look to Jesus Christ as our example and overcome sin and temptation as He overcame and was obedient unto death (1 John 5:3-6; Phil. 2:8).

God uses trials and hardships in our lives to produce a deeper faith and dependence on Him. These trials and hardships cause us to run to God for deliverance, who gives us the strength to get through each day. God also allows us to get into self-induced bondage so we can see how evil and unfulfilling it is, and so that we will repent and turn to Him for deliverance and restoration.

That the trial [a testing]¹ of your faith, being much more precious than of gold that perisheth, though it be tried with fire, might be found unto praise and honour and glory at the appearing of Jesus Christ.

—1 Peter 1:7

God uses all the hardships we go through to purify our faith by causing us to press further and deeper into a relationship with Jesus Christ. In turn, we receive more of His presence and empowerment to see things as they really are and to look past our circumstances to Him for our comfort, strength, and truth. He is continually showing us that He desires only obedient faith. The trials and tests that come to us throughout our lives are there to teach us to trust God no matter how bad things seem on the surface. He matures and purifies our faith throughout this process. A sign of mature faith is that we are not easily moved when things don't go exactly our way. Instead of getting angry and lashing out, we take it to God in prayer.

When we are tested, it shows us if our faith and trust in Jesus Christ and His Word is genuine. It's easy to trust God when everything is going our way! But when everything is going contrary to what we want, do we still trust Him? Or do we look to other people and the superficial things of this world for the answer to the unanswerable question of "why"? Yet most of the time we cannot answer that question until we are far removed from the situation. If we stayed steadfast and overcame the situation through our relationship with Jesus Christ (1 John 5:3-6), we would see how God used it for His glory. And if He shows us areas in our lives that caused the trials, it is for our good and betterment, so we will not go down that road again. The reality is that a lot of the trials we go through are self-induced through disobedience. We neglect our relationship with Jesus Christ and disobey His Word and allow all kinds of sin and bondage into our lives.

Of course there are numerous trials we go through that we did not cause, but the solution to overcome them are the same: "Nevertheless, not my will, but yours, be done" (Luke 22:42 ESV). We also will suffer numerous trials for our strong stance and testimony of Jesus Christ, but the Bible tells us to rejoice in those situations. "Blessed are ye, when men shall revile you, and persecute you, and shall say all manner of evil against you falsely, for my sake. Rejoice, and be exceeding glad: for great is your reward in heaven: for so persecuted they the prophets which were before you" (Matt. 5:11-12).

We need to learn from Jesus' experience in the Garden of Gethsemane, to look beyond our circumstances and trust that He will work everything out according to His perfect will, for our good and His glory. "The steps of a good man are ordered by the Lord: and he delighteth in his way" (Ps. 37: 23). That's exactly what Jesus did. He saw past His betrayal, beatings, and being mocked by those He came to save. He looked past enduring a slow excruciating death on the cross. What was He seeing, and why was it worth it to Him? He saw you and me living eternally in a joyous love relationship with Him. He also knew that good would come out of the whole situation only if He did (obeyed) His Father's will. It was well worth it to Him, and it is definitely worth it to us. That is why Jesus said, "Nevertheless, not my will, but yours, be done" (Luke 22:42 ESV).

And he cometh unto the disciples, and findeth them asleep, and he saith unto Peter, What, could ye not watch with me one hour? Watch and pray, that ye enter not into temptation: the spirit indeed is willing, but the flesh is weak. He went away again the second time, and prayed, saying, O my Father, if this cup may not pass away from me, except I drink it, thy will be done. And he came and found them asleep again: for their eyes were heavy. And he left them, and went away again, and prayed the third time, saying the same words. Then cometh he to his disciples, and saith unto them, Sleep on now, and take your rest: behold, the hour is at hand, and the Son of man is betrayed into the hands of sinners. Rise, let us be going: behold, he is at hand that doth betray me.

—Matthew 26:40-46

Jesus came back from His first prayer to find His disciples sleeping. He rebuked them by saying, "What, could ye not watch with me one hour?" Jesus was only away for one hour, and yet His disciples could not stay awake. Only one hour! Wasn't Jesus always there when the disciples needed Him? And now He needed His disciples to watch and pray with Him. Jesus had told them to "watch and pray," otherwise the night's events would take them by surprise and they would not be ready. Instead of watching and praying so that their faith would be strong and they would be prepared for what was about to happen, they did the opposite and did not resist temptation but succumbed to their own fleshly desires. The result was that they were caught off guard. They were not watching and praying, so naturally they allowed fear to enter into their hearts.

On this night, soldiers were on their way to arrest Jesus, led by one of His own disciples. But His disciples were oblivious to what was going to happen and were physically tired—so they slept. When Jesus returned, He told His disciples: "Watch and pray, that ye enter not into temptation: the spirit indeed is willing, but the flesh is weak." Then Jesus went away to pray a second time, and when He returned He found His disciples sleeping again. This time Jesus said nothing to His disciples and went a third and final time to pray to the Father. When He returned to His disciples, He told them to "Sleep on now, and take your rest: behold, the hour is at hand, and the Son of man is betrayed into the hands of sinners" (v.45). At this point Jesus knew that those who were coming to arrest Him were close, because He told His disciples: "Rise, let us be going: behold, he is at hand that doth betray me."

Instead of running from the situation, Jesus embraced the cross so that the Scriptures could be fulfilled. He met His betrayer and those who were with him to arrest Him so that He could get the upcoming events over with. While Jesus was being arrested, the disciples were overcome by the night's events and didn't know quite what to do. They were surprised, confused, and afraid and did not know what to do next. Mark 14:50 tells us that the disciples "all left him and fled" (ESV). So the disciples, full of fear, were overcome by the night's events and ran away and hid.

> Now the chief priests and the whole Council were seeking testimony against Jesus to put him to death, but they found none. For many bore false witness against him, but their testimony did not agree.
>
> —Mark 14:55-56 (ESV)

Later on that night when Jesus was brought before the High Priest, Peter followed at a safe distance into the courtyard of the High Priest. During Peter's time in the courtyard, many false witnesses were accusing Jesus and none of those witnesses agreed with each other. Peter never stepped forward during this time to defend Jesus, even though He could have easily discredited those false witnesses. Peter knew Jesus better than anyone there, for he had spent the last three years with Him.

In fact, Peter denied being a disciple of Jesus Christ when confronted by those in the courtyard. When Peter denied being Christ's disciple three times, he recalled the words Jesus had spoke to him: "Before the cock crow twice, thou shalt deny me thrice. And when he [Peter] thought thereon, he wept" (Mark 14:72). None of the disciples including Peter were prepared for what was going to happen to Jesus, even though He had told them and prepared them for it. The disciples did not believe Jesus and were overconfident in their faith, which had not been tested. When Jesus had told Peter that he was going to deny Him, Peter denied it and "said emphatically, 'If I must die with you, I will not deny you.' And they [the disciples] all said the same" (Mark 14:31 ESV). But they all ended up denying Him when their faith was tested.

At this point, the disciples felt guilty and scared and did not know what to do—so they went into hiding. But Jesus did not leave His disciples in this state, for He loved them. After the resurrection, Jesus visited His disciples numerous times. He wanted to prove to them that He had resurrected and that everything He said would come to pass, did. "To them he presented himself alive after his suffering by many proofs, appearing to them during forty days speaking about the kingdom of God" (Acts 1:3 ESV). He also wanted to show them that He had fulfilled every one of the prophecies concerning Him. He wanted to rid them of their unbelief and propel them into the world as His witnesses. They were eyewitnesses from the beginning of Jesus' earthly ministry on through His death and resurrection. No one knew Jesus better than His disciples.

Then he said to them, "These are my words that I spoke to you while I was still with you, that everything written about me in the Law of Moses and the Prophets and the Psalms must be fulfilled." Then he opened their minds to understand the Scriptures, and said to them, "Thus it is written, that the Christ should suffer and on the third day rise from the dead, and that repentance and forgiveness of sins should be proclaimed in his name to all nations, beginning from Jerusalem. You are witnesses of these things.

—Luke 24:44-48 (ESV)

The disciples failed their test of faith because they were relying on their own strength and resolve. They were not dependent on their relationship with Jesus Christ in Word and prayer for their strength, plus they had not been given the Holy Spirit yet. They needed to discard any confidence in their own abilities, as well as any preconceived notions on how Jesus was to establish His kingdom. They needed the Holy Spirit in their lives to lead them, to illuminate the truth of God's Word, and to give them the boldness and the power to witness. That is why when Jesus was still physically with them, He told them: "It is expedient for you that I go away: for if I go not away, the Comforter [Holy Spirit] will not come unto you; but if I depart, I will send him unto you. And when he is come, he will reprove the world of sin, and of righteousness, and of judgment.… Howbeit when he, the Spirit of truth, is come, he will guide you into all truth: for he shall not speak of himself; but whatsoever he shall hear, that shall ye speak: and he will shew you things to come. He shall glorify me: for he shall receive of mine, and shall shew it unto you. All things that the Father hath are mine: therefore said I, that he shall take of mine, and shew it unto you" (John 16:7-8, 13-15).

After the resurrection, Jesus appeared multiple times during a 40-day period to His disciples, making sure they knew that He was alive. He made sure they understood all the Scriptures concerning Him, so that they could be effective witnesses for Him. He also wanted them to know that He would be with them and guide them in a different way than He had in the past three years. He was going to lead them, work with them, and work through them by His Spirit. Most of all, they would always recognize that He was present in their lives.

That is why Jesus said that it was good that He goes away so He could send the promised Holy Spirit into their lives. One of the last instructions Jesus gave to His disciples in those 40 days would change their faith forever. Jesus told them in Luke 24:49: "I send the promise of my Father upon you: but tarry ye in the city of Jerusalem, until ye be endued with power from on high." Jesus told them to wait in Jerusalem until they were filled with the Holy Spirit. The disciples—no longer trusting in themselves or wanting to do things their own way—obeyed Jesus and waited in Jerusalem for the promise. They were totally convinced that Jesus was the resurrected Messiah and, unlike the night in the Garden of Gethsemane, they wanted to obey Him.

So the disciples obeyed Jesus' command and waited in Jerusalem. "These all continued with one accord in prayer and supplication, with the women, and Mary the Mother of Jesus, and with his brethren" (Acts 1:14). They were assembled together watching and praying and waiting for the promised Holy Spirit. They were willing to watch and wait at this point, because they did not want to miss what the Lord had for them; they wanted to be prepared for it.

When the day of Pentecost arrived, they were all together in one place. And suddenly there came from heaven a sound like a mighty

rushing wind, and it filled the entire house where they were sitting.
And divided tongues as of fire appeared to them and rested on each
one of them. And they were all filled with the Holy Spirit and began
to speak in other tongues as the Spirit gave them utterance.

—Acts 2:1-4 (ESV)

After the disciples were filled with the Holy Spirit, their ministry changed. They had a newfound power in their lives. They were no longer timid and afraid and were filled with faith. They had power and spoke with authority and boldness. Jesus was no longer one person on the earth, but now He inhabited every one of His disciples and every born again (regenerated) believer. From this point on, the disciples gave themselves to prayer, studying of God's Word, and preaching. As a result, the church grew daily and the disciples performed many miracles (Acts 2:47). After Peter's first sermon, 3,000 souls were saved (Acts 2:41). They had completely changed and were no longer relying on their own strength but on Christ's. They daily yielded their lives over to the Holy Spirit and had no problem waiting and watching in prayer as they did on that dreadful night in the garden. As a matter of fact, the disciples were spending their days and nights totally focused on fulfilling the Lord's will.

The disciples didn't dwell on their past failures; they made every moment count for the kingdom of God. They spread the gospel from Jerusalem to distant lands, no longer fearing what man could do to them. These disciples left families, homes, and jobs to preach to the world that Jesus was the Son of God and had resurrected. They were totally convinced that Jesus was the Son of God and that everything about Him was true. They were so convinced that they laid down their lives for Jesus Christ.

The Disciples Gave Everything for Their Lord[2]

1. Peter—crucified upside down on a cross

2. Philip—crucified

3. Simon—crucified

4. Bartholomew—crucified

5. Andrew—crucified

6. James, son of Zebedee—beheaded

7. James, son of Alphaeus—stoned to death

8. Jude or Judas (not Iscariot the betrayer) or called Thaddeus—crucified

9. Matthew—slain with an halberd (weapon with an ax-like cutting blade)

10. Thomas—speared to death

11. Matthias (Judas Iscariot's replacement)—stoned and then beheaded

12. John, exiled to the Island of Patmos for the "Word of God, and for the testimony of Jesus Christ" (Rev 1:9)—died of old age

Jesus' resisted the temptation to avoid and disobey His Father's will to die on the cross. He instead chose to lay down His life as a living sacrifice for us, fulfilling and obeying God's Word. That night in the Garden of Gethsemane was a night of testing for Jesus and for all of His disciples. The word "Gethsemane" means "Olive Press."[3] Olives were brought to the olive press to be crushed in order to extract the olive oil that was used for so many things during that time period. The olives were put into a rock cistern and were either crushed by a millstone or by human feet.[4] The olives had to be totally crushed or stomped down to nothing in order to squeeze out all the olive oil. Once the oil was extracted, it had to be strained (cleaned) in order to get all of the impurities out. The whole form of the olive had to be changed radically to get the precious olive oil.

Jesus had to go through the "press" in order to be our perfect sacrifice and our resurrected Lord. He was whipped, beaten, humiliated, mocked, nailed to a cross, and suffered excruciating pain. He went through all this in order to take our punishment for sin and make a way for us to have eternal life through Him. Jesus got through the "press" by being totally obedient to the Father's will, because He was totally dependent on Him. "And being found in fashion as a man, he humbled himself, and became obedient unto death, even the death of the cross" (Phil. 2:8).

Before the disciples went through the "press," they succumbed to the temptation to look out for themselves instead of taking their directions from Jesus. They were not ready because they were not obeying Jesus' direction to "watch and pray." They were not yet totally dependent on Jesus and were self-confident and self-sufficient. As long as everything was going right, they were faithful disciples. Jesus had told them what would happen, but they had their own ideas and plans apart from God's will.

Ultimately, Jesus had to put His disciples through the "press" to show them their faith and to get rid of those things in their lives that would hinder Him from working through them. They were hindered by their lack of faith in Him, the direct result of a prayerless life. They were relying on their own strength as well as their own preconceived plans and ideas— they were not totally dependent on Him. The "press" exposed their hearts and brought them to the end of themselves, so they would no longer look to themselves but to Him. After going through the "press," they wanted nothing from themselves. They gladly welcomed the Holy Spirit into their lives to empower them. They wanted to know and serve Christ and be filled with His Spirit. They no longer trusted in their own faith but pursued the One who produces genuine faith. The rest is history!

For we have not an high priest which cannot be touched with the feeling of our infirmities; but was in all points tempted like as we are, yet without sin. Let us therefore come boldly unto the throne of grace, that we may obtain mercy, and find grace to help in time of need.

—Hebrews 4:15-16

It is important for us to know that no matter what desperate situation we are facing, Jesus understands and sympathizes with us. He is our great High Priest waiting to answer our prayers and to pour out His Spirit to enable us to endure, resist, and overcome. Don't think for a second that Jesus does not hear our desperate cry for strength and help. It is quite the opposite, having been desperate Himself in the Garden of Gethsemane—He understands that cry! If we disregard our own desires and yield our situation to His will, He will see us through.

Jesus Christ our High Priest intercedes (prays) for us according to the Father's will (Heb. 7:25). He sympathizes with our troubles and was tempted like we are; yet He did not sin (4:15). But all this means nothing in our lives unless we obey verse 16. "Let us therefore come boldly unto the throne of grace, that we may obtain mercy, and find grace to help in time of need." We need His life and power within us to enable us to go through the "press" with the faith that will triumph through it!

Who is it that is victorious over [that conquers] the world but he who believes that Jesus is the Son of God [who adheres to, trusts in, and relies on that fact]? This is He Who came by (with) water and blood [His baptism and His death], Jesus Christ (the Messiah).

—1 John 5:5-6 (AMP)

CHAPTER 2

▼

ASK AND KEEP ON ASKING! SEEK AND KEEP ON SEEKING!

But without faith it is impossible to please him: for he that cometh to God must believe that he is, and that he is a rewarder of them that diligently seek Him.

—Hebrews 11:6

The faith we will be talking about in this chapter is a faith that pleases God. This is the only faith we are to have. Our society and even modern Christianity has different interpretations on what it means to "have faith." Faith is not a superficial one-time acknowledgement of a perceived truth or something you can have without obedience. It is something we cannot espouse to have without it manifesting in our lives (James 2:17-20). Faith is also something we cannot generate ourselves; it comes through our love relationship with Jesus Christ. Jesus shows His love for us by His actions and regenerates our hearts towards Him, so we in turn reciprocate this love He has for us by loving Him. Because we love Him and know His way is perfect, we in turn desire to live our lives according to His will. Therefore we believe His Word is true by acting upon it.

Unfortunately, it is popular in our society to say, "I believe in Jesus and have faith in Him," while living lives in complete opposition and rebellion towards Him. This is not what the Bible defines as faith or belief. This is certainly not saving faith! God does not regenerate our hearts to serve ourselves but to serve Him. Saving faith is manifested in a heart that loves Him and wants more of Him. It manifests in a person who knows and believes that Jesus Christ is the solution to all their needs, whether spiritual or physical.

If you [really] love Me, you will keep (obey) My commands.
—John 14:15 (AMP)

If a person has faith in Jesus Christ, it means that person loves Him. "Faith which worketh by love" (Gal. 5:6). The Bible tells us that if we love Him, we will obey Him. Obedience is a natural result of a relationship with Jesus Christ. A person who has been "born again" by His Spirit, (John 3:3) will no longer live for himself but for Him (Rom. 6:6). He will live an obedient life in his pursuit of knowing Jesus Christ. He will never be satisfied with where he's at in his faith but will be wanting continually more of Jesus Christ in his life. He will seek Jesus Christ with all that is in him! He will never be comfortable sinning against God and you won't hear him justifying sin in his life or in the lives of others.

I have had people tell me that faith is personnel, and should not be discussed openly. It is true that our relationship with Jesus Christ is personnel and in the end we will stand before Him alone. But faith that can stay hidden is a false faith or no faith at all. For when a person has faith, it will be manifest to all! That person's number one desire will be to know Jesus Christ, and it will be manifested in everything he does.

That is why in Hebrews 11:6 it says: "without faith it is impossible to please him." Why? Because "he that cometh to God must believe that he is" who He says He is.

Who is He?

1. "All things were made by him; and without him was not anything made" (John 1:3).

2. "He is the author and finisher of our faith" (Heb. 12:2).

3. "God so loved the world, that he gave us his only begotten Son" (John 3:16).

4. "While we were yet sinners, Christ died for us" (Rom. 5:8).

5. He sympathizes with our weaknesses (Heb. 4:15).

6. Salvation and eternal life are through Jesus Christ (John 1:12; 3:16; 5:24-25; 11:25; Acts 3:19; 11:25; Rom. 10:9-13).

7. He is our healer (1 Peter 2:24).

8. He became sin for us, even though He had no sin, so that we could be made righteous before God (2 Cor. 5:21).

9. "If we confess our sins, he is faithful and just to forgive us our sins, and to cleanse us from all unrighteousness" (1 John 1:9).

10. If we confess our sins, He does not remember them anymore (Isa. 43:25).

11. We have peace with God, by being justified by faith in Jesus Christ (Rom. 3:24; 5:1).

12. He rewards those that diligently seek Him (Heb. 11:6).

These are just a few things that describe who God is. We must believe that God is who He says He is, otherwise we would not seek Him. We must believe that God's Word is true, or otherwise we would not follow it. We must believe that Jesus died on the cross for our sins and through Him we have forgiveness of sins and a new life. "Therefore, if anyone is in Christ, he is a new creation. The old has passed away; behold, the new has come" (2 Cor. 5:17 ESV). So, if we profess that we have faith in Jesus Christ but do not manifest that faith in our lives, it surely is a false faith. If we had faith in Jesus Christ, we would "hunger and thirst" for more of Him (Matt. 5:6). We would want to glorify Him in every aspect of our lives.

Not only do we need to believe who God says He is, but we need to believe what God says about us.

1. "For all have sinned, and come short of the glory of God" (Rom. 3:23).

2. "All our righteous deeds are like a polluted garment" (Isa. 64:6 ESV).

3. "There is none righteous, no, not one" (Rom. 3:10).

4. "Death passed upon all men, for that all have sinned" (Rom. 5:12).

5. "For the wages of sin is death; but the gift of God is eternal life through Jesus Christ our Lord" (Rom. 6:23).

6. "Whosoever was not found written in the book of life was cast into the lake of fire" (Rev. 20:15).

7. "He that hath the Son hath life: and he that hath not the Son of God hath not life" (1 John 5:12).

We need to know that we are sinners destined to go to hell unless we repent and turn our lives over to Jesus Christ's direction, and that in our best state we are altogether sinners and our lives are unacceptable before God. No person is accepted by God who is a sinner (unholy). God only accepts us through our relationship with Jesus Christ. God only accepts the righteousness of Jesus Christ, and those who are in Christ are accepted by Him. We have to believe what the Bible tells us—we are wretched and without hope apart from Jesus Christ. We have to believe who He is and who He says we are, or we will never want to have the faith we need.

This brings us to the last part of Hebrews 11:6: "He is a rewarder of them that diligently seek him." That is why faith pleases God. Because if we truly believe in Him and the promises that He has given us in His Word, we would diligently seek Him for those promises to be manifested in our lives. The more faith we have in Jesus Christ, the more dependent we will be on the Holy Spirit's direction and help and the greater our prayer life will be.

That is why He rewards those who diligently seek Him. Be who know Him will seek Him and will not give up until the ans erance, healing, or revelation comes. He loves and rewards tha faith because the people praying believe whole-heartedly that He wants to answer their prayers. They also believe that He is the o who can answer their prayers and are desperate for Him to do learned from Jesus' Gethsemane experience that He is in tune to tha perate cry. He was there and experienced it Himself.

The Bible gives us numerous examples of persevering faith. When I the term "persevering faith," I mean that God has spoken to us throu His Word, and we obey it no matter what things look like in our lives. We persevere in prayer for the Lord to give us the strength to wait for His Word to come to fruition, and we obey Him in the process. If we are not persevering in prayer, we will allow unbelief and doubt to enter in. When we allow this to happen, then we naturally pray less, because we will no longer believe that He answers prayers. But if we stand upon His Word and pray according to His will, we will get what we ask for. "And all things, whatsoever ye shall ask in prayer, believing, ye shall receive" (Matt. 21:22).

In the next few pages, we will look at numerous examples of persevering faith. First, we will look at two people who went to great lengths to get Jesus' attention and who would not give up until their desperate prayers were answered. Then we will look at two New Testament parables Jesus gave us to show us how we are to persevere in prayer.

The Official's Sick Son

So he came again to Cana in Galilee, where he had made the water wine. And at Capernaum there was an official whose son was ill. When this man heard that Jesus had come from Judea to Galilee, he went to him and asked him to come down and heal his son, for he was at the point of death. So Jesus said to him, "Unless you see signs and wonders you will not believe." The official said to him, "Sir, come down before my child dies." Jesus said to him, "Go; your son will live." The man believed the word Jesus spoke to him and went on his way. As he was going down, his servants met him and told him that his son was recovering. So he asked them the hour when he began to get better, and they said to him, "Yesterday at the seventh hour the fever left him." The father knew that was the hour when Jesus had said to him, "Your son will live." And he himself believed, and all his household.

—John 4:46-53 (ESV)

Here we have the story of an official living in Capernaum whose son was very ill. The Scriptures describe his son's condition as being at the "point of death." The official had heard that Jesus of Nazareth had come from Judea to Cana of Galilee, so he set out to find Him. You know he was desperate, because he was willing to leave his son for a few days to seek Jesus. Capernaum was over 15 miles away from Cana of Galilee,[1] and in those days people walked everywhere they went. It most likely took the official a day and a half to reach Jesus.

Jesus' reputation had spread throughout the land. So when the official heard where Jesus was located, he was willing to leave his son, who could die any day, to pursue Jesus. The official did not send someone else to talk to Jesus, even though he was an important man in Capernaum. No, he set out to get the answer he needed for himself. We can only imagine that he had tried every kind of medical treatment and medicine that were available at the time. A man of his importance probably could obtain the best doctors available to cure his son. But, to no avail. Jesus was his only hope.

On his way to see Jesus, the official's total concentration and thoughts were on Jesus healing his son. The official did not give in to the fact that his son was dying. He didn't just wish that his son would get better. No, he did not! He didn't just say a few prayers and give it to God. He pursued Jesus until He found Him, and then kept petitioning Him until he got what he was praying for.

You know that the official's heart was pounding when he saw Jesus. He was desperate for Jesus to work a miracle in his situation. All his hopes, all his dreams, and all his future were riding on Jesus. The son that he loved so much, had plans for, and would carry on his name—he had to live!

When he approached Jesus, he asked Him to come to his house and heal his son. Jesus responded by saying, "Unless you see signs and wonders you will not believe." Jesus' response was probably due to the fact that He discerned that the official wanted some kind of sign and needed assurance that his son would be healed. Maybe in the official's mind, he thought that if Jesus went with him to his house, this would be a clear sign that his son would be healed. So Jesus showed him what was in his heart by exposing it. Jesus did this to strengthen the man's faith by teaching him not to look for "signs or wonders," but to just believe.

The official, more desperate than ever and not willing to give up, said a second time to Jesus: "Sir, come down before my child dies." Jesus answered his prayer, but not like the official was hoping, for he wanted Jesus to go with him. Jesus told him, "Go; your son will live." The official then believed the words Jesus spoke and obeyed Him and left. The official went home having no sign or physical assurance other than the assurance of Jesus' words: "Your son will live." He believed Jesus' words and went home with the expectation that his son was healed.

The official's trip home must have felt never ending. You know he was extremely eager to get home to see his son. There might have been some doubts in his mind on that long, quiet road back home. But he believed Jesus' word, because that is all he had. Ultimately, he found out that Jesus' word would be all he would ever need. For the next day he was met by some of his servants who gave him the good news that his son was recovering. The official asked them what hour his son started to get better. His servants told him: "Yesterday at the seventh hour [1 p.m.] the fever left him." The official knew that was the same hour when Jesus had told him: "Your son will live." He believed Jesus, and so did everyone in his household.

Blind Bartimaeus

And they came to Jericho. And as he was leaving Jericho with his disciples and a great crowd, Bartimaeus, a blind beggar, the son of Timaeus, was sitting by the roadside. And when he heard that it was Jesus of Nazareth, he began to cry out and say, "Jesus, Son of David, have mercy on me!" And many rebuked him, telling him to be silent. But he cried out all the more, "Son of David, have mercy on me!" And Jesus stopped and said, "Call him." And they called the blind man, saying to him, "Take heart. Get up; he is calling you." And throwing off his cloak, he sprang up and came to Jesus. And Jesus said to him, "What do you want me to do for you?" And the blind man said to him, "Rabbi, let me recover my sight." And Jesus said to him, "Go your way; your faith has made you well." And immediately he recovered his sight and followed him on the way.

—Mark 10:46-53 (ESV)

As Jesus was leaving Jericho with His disciples, a great crowd of people followed Him. As they walked, they passed a "blind beggar" named Bartimaeus sitting by the side of the road. He could not see, but could hear the large crowd passing by. When he heard that it was Jesus of Nazareth walking by, "he began to cry out and say, 'Jesus, Son of David, have mercy on me!'" The passage says: "he began to cry out." He was so aggressive in his calling out to Jesus that the people around him tried to shut him up. He didn't listen to them, but cried out even harder. "Son of David, have mercy on me!" This time, Jesus heard him and stopped and said, "Call him."

Bartimaeus spent his life begging because he was blind. He did not have food or money unless people gave it to him, and they would not give him those things unless he aggressively begged for it. That is probably why he was so aggressive in his calling out to Jesus. He did not care what other people thought. He was not going to let other people get in the way of him getting Jesus' attention. He wanted to be healed of his blindness, and he knew that Jesus could do it. He could not see Jesus to go after him, so he cried out. He was so relentless in his calling out that he got Jesus' attention. Jesus stopped and called for him.

If Bartimaeus had not relentlessly cried out, or if he had listened to the people around him and remained silent, Jesus would have walked by. Finally, he had Jesus' attention. The people told him, "Get up; he is calling you." Jesus was calling him and he had a voice to go to. So he threw off his cloak, because he did not want anything slowing him down, and "he sprang up" ("jumped up" NASB) and came to Jesus. Bartimaeus knew that nothing was more important than talking face to face with Jesus Christ.

When he got to Jesus, He asked him, "What do you want me to do for you?" He wanted Bartimaeus to be specific in his request. Bartimaeus said, "Rabbi [my master], let me recover my sight." Jesus answered his request and told him, "Go your way; your faith has made you well." Immediately his sight was restored and he began to follow Jesus.

We can see from these two examples that these men relentlessly pursued Jesus. They didn't give up until they received what they petitioned for. These examples in the Bible are written for us, so that we can learn from them. Today we do not have Jesus physically with us, but He is spiritually with us. We don't have to take a journey to His location, or call out to Him through a crowd for Him to hear us and answer our prayer. But we should pursue Christ with the same intensity in our prayer life. Remember, He rewards those who diligently seek Him! Just as the official spent a few days focused on getting to Jesus, we must spend ample time in prayer with our requests. Sometimes it takes days, months, and even years for our prayers to be answered, but He will answer those prayers, for He rewards those who diligently seek Him.

We cannot expect anything from the Lord if we are not seeking Him in prayer. If He rewards those who *diligently* seek Him, then there is no reward for those who don't. Those who do not diligently seek Him, do not believe in Jesus Christ. If they truly knew Jesus Christ and believed His Word, they would hunger and thirst for more of Him and diligently seek Him (Matt. 5:6). Through their diligence in seeking Him, they would have more of His presence in their lives. This presence would give them the power to overcome and resist sin. They would also know His Word and believe it and pray effectively because they would be praying according to His will (John 15:7). As their relationship with Jesus Christ grows, they will naturally increase in their desire and intensity to pray.

Jesus also gave us numerous parables in the New Testament reinforcing the kind of perseverance that He expects from those who believe. Those who believe are expected to pray and be effective in their pursuits. We'll now look at two parables Jesus taught on prayer.

The Persistent Friend

Then He said to them, "Suppose one of you has a friend, and goes to him at midnight and says to him, 'Friend, lend me three loaves; for a friend of mine has come to me from a journey, and I have nothing to set before him'; and from inside he answers and says, 'Do not bother me; the door has already been shut and my children and I are in bed; I cannot get up and give you anything.' I tell you, even though he will not get up and give him anything because he is his friend, yet because of his persistence he will get up and give him as much as he needs. So I say to you, ask, and it will be given unto you; seek, and you will find; knock, and it will be opened unto you. For everyone who asks, receives; and he who seeks, finds; and to him who knocks, it will be opened. Now suppose one of you fathers is asked by his son for a fish; he will not give him a snake instead of a fish, will he? Or if he is asked for an egg, he will not give him a scorpion, will he? If you then, being evil, know how to give good gifts to your children, how much more will your heavenly Father give the Holy Spirit to those who ask Him?"

—Luke 11:5-13 (NASB)

It is important to know that Jesus gave His disciples this parable right after He taught them the Lord's Prayer. Luke 11 starts out with Jesus praying, and when He had stopped, one of His disciples approached Him and asked, "Lord, teach us to pray" (v.1). So Jesus taught them the Lord's Prayer as a model for all their prayers.

Our Father which art in heaven, hallowed be thy name. Thy kingdom come. Thy will be done, as in heaven, so in earth. Give us day by day our daily bread. And forgive us our sins; for we also forgive every one that is indebted to us. And lead us not into temptation; but deliver us from evil.

—Luke 11:2-4

The prayer model Jesus gave teaches us how we are to pray. First we need to put God in His rightful place by worshiping and honoring Him: "Hallowed be thy name." Next we need to put His kingdom and His will above our own needs: "Thy kingdom come. Thy will be done." We are to earnestly pray that His will is done in our lives as well as in the lives of others and that His kingdom is manifested on the earth. Then we are to pray for our personnel needs according to His divine will. He even teaches us how to do this. We are to pray for our daily necessities, like food. We are to pray for the forgiveness of sins, making sure that we have forgiven everyone that has wronged us. We are to pray for the power to overcome temptation and to be delivered from evil.

Right after Jesus taught His disciples the Lord's Prayer, He gave them the parable of the persistent friend. This persistent friend came to his friend's house at midnight and wanted some food. His friend responded by saying, "Do not bother me; my door has already been shut and my children and I are in bed; I cannot get up and give you anything." Then to bring home the point of the parable, Jesus says, "I tell you, even though he will not get up and give him anything because he is his friend, yet because of his persistence he will get up and give him as much as he needs." Because of his persistence, the friend will get up and give him food. If he doesn't, he knows he will be bothered all night long until he gives his friend what he wants.

That is the kind of perseverance we are to have in our prayer life, and that's the kind of persistence in prayer that Jesus is teaching us in this parable. Jesus ends this parable with an exhortation to ask and keep on asking and to seek and to keep on seeking! "So I say to you, ask, and it will be given unto you; seek, and you will find; knock and it will be opened unto you. For everyone who asks, receives; and he who seeks, finds; and to him who knocks, it will be opened." This persistent friend needed food and knew that his friend had what he needed and did not give up until he got what he wanted.

Imagine if you needed food and you knew a person who had plenty. In your desperation, you would knock, beg, and pester that person for food until you received it. That is how we are to be in our prayer life. No matter what our situation is or our desperate need, God is in control and will answer our need.

The Unjust Judge

And he [Jesus] spake a parable unto them to this end, that men ought always to pray, and not to faint; saying, There was in a city a judge, which feared not God, neither regarded man: and there was a widow in that city; and she came unto him, saying, Avenge me of mine adversary. And he would not for a while: but afterward he said within himself, Though I fear not God, nor regard man; yet because this widow troubleth me, I will avenge her, lest by her continual coming she weary me. And the Lord said, Hear what the unjust judge saith. And shall not God avenge his own elect, which cry day and night unto him, though he bear long with them? I tell you that he will avenge them speedily. Nevertheless when the son of man cometh, shall he find faith on the earth?

—Luke 18:1-8

This is another parable Jesus gave us on perseverance. Jesus said, "Men ought always to pray, and not to faint." We should persevere in prayer and not grow tired or give up. The unjust judge didn't care about the widow's request, but he answered because he didn't want to keep being bothered by her. The unjust judge knew that she would not give up until she received justice. So he ruled in her favor because he did not want to be worn down by her continual coming to him. If this is how an unjust judge, who does not care about the situation at all, answers, how much more will a loving God answer our prayers?

Then Jesus said, "And shall God not avenge his own elect, which cry day and night unto him." This is the true test to see if someone has persevering faith: They cry out day and night to the Lord. They cry out knowing that God hears them, convinced that He is the solution. If the unjust judge answered the widow's petition, how much more will a loving heavenly Father who loves us answer our prayers?

Only the Holy Spirit can convict a person of sin and bring him to repentance. I have seen such changes in people that I have prayed for over the years. For some people it has been a sudden change, others have been gradual. Then I have prayed for others for years, and still I have seen no change. I am learning to not look at the natural, because the Word tells us if we pray according to His will, He will answer our prayers (John 15:7). We might not see it right away, but He will. Prayer builds faith, and the more faith we have the more we will pray.

And whatsoever we ask, we receive of him, because we keep his commandments, and do those things that are pleasing in his sight. And this is his commandment, That we should believe on the name of his Son Jesus Christ, and love one another, as he gave us commandment.

—1 John 3:22-23

The Bible tells us that as we love others by praying for them, He will answer our prayers. When we do not pray for self-centered reasons to fulfill our own lusts and our own agenda, He will answer our prayers. Obviously, if we are living a sinful and rebellious life, not desiring a relationship with Jesus Christ, He will not answer our prayers. "If I regard iniquity in my heart, the Lord will not hear me" (Ps. 66:18).

Why? Because He first wants us to get rid of those things in our lives that hinder our relationship with Him. Everything starts with our relationship with Jesus Christ and spills over from that. Even if we are not praying according to His will, He will reveal it to us and direct our prayers according to His will. Through intercession, we will gain His heart and intercede according to His will. We should never give up praying for those who we think are a lost cause or have no hope, nor should we give up praying for people when the answer does not come right away.

No one is too far gone for Jesus Christ not to change, deliver, and heal. Multitudes of people have been healed from all kinds of terminal diseases and life-controlling problems. The people we might think are too far gone or too messed up, might just be the ones God will use mightily.

Just as God does not give up on people, we should keep persevering in prayer for others. But most of all, we need to continually pray that God would do a deeper work in our lives, produce a greater faith, and make us yielded vessels filled with His Spirit so that we manifest His life and truth in everything we do. We need to pray for a hunger to have a deeper intimacy with Jesus Christ so that we would hear His voice, know His will, and pray according to His will.

Nothing is impossible with God. If we want our situation to change, we need to persevere in prayer. If we want the people around us to change, we need to persevere in prayer. He has given us so many examples in His Word where people persisted with their requests and Jesus answered them. When we pray, we are in communion with Him and He transforms us in the process. In that transformation, we gain His heart and pray according to His will for specific situations. Prayer also gives us discernment and insight into certain situations we're dealing with. God might not change our situation the way we think it should change, but He may change how we deal with that situation.

It is paramount in our Christian walk to pray, because we gain so much from it. We gain intimacy with Jesus Christ, discernment, faith, God's will, and the answer to our prayers. It is the best and most important form of worship we can give to God. One cannot have a relationship with the Lord without prayer. Prayer is obedience to the Lord and proves our dependence on Him.

In this nation, people will spend hours training for a sport and persevering through hard training to reach their goal. Or they will persevere to get a project done at work because they know it will pay off monetarily. But for some reason, people will not persevere in prayer to change their lives or for the salvation of a loved one. People will not persevere for physical healing or the healing of our nation. Why is that? Is it because we really don't believe what God has told us? If we do not persevere in prayer, our faith is weak. Unfortunately for most people, prayer is the last resort. They only turn to prayer if they cannot work their problems out on their own. Prayer should be, instead, the first and final resort.

CHAPTER 3

▼

THE PROPHET'S DISOBEDIENCE

And he went after the man of God and found him sitting under an oak. And he said to him, "Are you the man of God who came from Judah?" And he said, "I am." Then he said to him, "Come home with me and eat bread." And he said, "I may not return with you, or go in with you, neither will I eat bread nor drink water with you in this place, for it was said to me by the word of the LORD, 'You shall neither eat bread nor drink water there, nor return by the way that you came.'" And he said to him, "I also am a prophet as you are, and an angel spoke to me by the word of the LORD, saying, 'Bring him back with you into your house that he may eat bread and drink water.'" But he lied to him. So he went back with him and ate bread in his house and drank water. And as they sat at the table, the word of the LORD came to the prophet who had brought him back. And he cried to the man of God who came from Judah, "Thus says the LORD, 'Because you have disobeyed the word of the LORD and have not kept the command that the LORD your God commanded you, but have come back and have eaten bread and drunk water in the place of which he said to you, "Eat no bread and drink no water," your body shall not come to the tomb of your fathers.'" And after he had eaten bread and drunk, he saddled the donkey for the prophet whom he had brought back. And as he went away a lion met him on the road and killed him.

—1 Kings 13:14-24 (ESV)

King Solomon reigned in Jerusalem over all of Israel for forty years. When Solomon died, he was buried in the City of David and his son Rehoboam reigned in his place. One of the first things Rehoboam did as king was to go to Shechem, for all of Israel came there to officially make him king. During this time, there was a man named Jeroboam who was living in Egypt because he had fled from King Solomon. Now that King Solomon was dead and his son Rehoboam had taken his place, he returned to Israel.

The people sent and called for Jeroboam to come to Shechem. Jeroboam and all of Israel came together to talk to Rehoboam. They said to Rehoboam: "Your father made our yoke heavy. Now therefore lighten the hard service of your father and his heavy yoke on us, and we will serve you" (1 Kings 12:4 ESV). The people of Israel had been burdened down with work under King Solomon, and now that he was dead they appealed to his son to lessen the workload. Rehoboam told the people to go away for three days and come back to him, and he would give them an answer.

King Rehoboam sought council with the old men that had advised his father. They told him: "If you will be a servant to this people today and serve them, and speak good words to them when you answer them, then they will be your servants forever" (v.7). But Rehoboam did not listen to them; instead he sought council from the friends he had grown up with. They told him not to lessen the people's burden, but to treat them even worse by adding to their burden. So when Jeroboam and all the people came to Rehoboam on the third day, the king "answered the people harshly" (v.13). "'My father made your yoke heavy, but I will add to your yoke. My father disciplined you with whips, but I will discipline you with scorpions.' So the king did not listen to the people"
(1 Kings 12:14-15 ESV).

When the people of Israel saw that the king did not listen to them, they told him: "What portion do we have in David? We have no inheritance in the son of Jesse" (v.16), and they went back home. From that point on,

Israel was split. Rehoboam ruled over the people of Israel that lived in the cities of Judah. The rest of the people of Israel made Jeroboam their king. Only the tribes of Judah and Benjamin followed the house of David (Rehoboam).

When Rehoboam returned to Jerusalem, he assembled men from the tribes of Judah and Benjamin to fight against Israel to restore the kingdom back. "But the word of God came to Shemaiah the man of God: 'Say to Rehoboam the son of Solomon, king of Judah, and to all the house of Judah and Benjamin, and to the rest of the people, 'Thus says the LORD, you shall not go up or fight against your relatives the people of Israel. Every man return to his home, for this thing is from me.' So they listened to the word of the LORD and went home again, according to the word of the LORD" (1 Kings 12:23-24).

Rehoboam and the men of Judah and Benjamin obeyed God and returned home.

The temple of the Lord in Jerusalem was the only place in all of Israel that sacrifices could be made before the Lord. That area belonged to Rehoboam the King of Judah. Jeroboam was worried that his people would go to Jerusalem to make their sacrifices and their hearts would turn again to the Lord and to Rehoboam the King of Judah. So Jeroboam made two golden calves and set one in Bethel and the other in Dan. Jeroboam said to the people: "You have gone up to Jerusalem long enough. Behold your gods, O Israel, who brought you up out of the land of Egypt" (1 Kings 12:28). He also set up temples on high places and appointed priests from the people who were not Levites. The men of the tribe of Levi were the only ones designated by God to be priests. Jeroboam disregarded that. He totally fabricated his own religion appointing his own priest and even instituted a feast on the fifteenth day of the eighth month just as Judah had. He did what all false religions do: he tried to mimic the rituals and the traditions but switched out the god.

Jeroboam went up to the altar he had made in Bethel on the fifteenth day of the eighth month to make offerings to the golden calf. When Jeroboam was at the altar, a man came out of Judah who was sent by God. "And the man cried against the altar by the word of the LORD and said, 'O altar, altar, thus says the LORD: "Behold, a son shall be born to the house of David, Josiah by name, and he shall sacrifice on you the priests of the high places who make offerings on you, and human bones shall be burned on you.'" And he gave a sign the same day, saying, 'This is the sign that the LORD has spoken: "Behold, the altar shall be torn down, and the ashes that are on it shall be poured out"'" (1 Kings 13:2-3 ESV).

When the king heard what the man of God said against the altar of Bethel, he reached out to grab him while telling the others to "Seize him." As soon as Jeroboam stretched out his hand against the man of God, it dried up and the altar was torn down and the ashes poured out, according to the sign the man of God by the word of the Lord had given. When Jeroboam saw his hand, he petitioned the man of God: "'Entreat now the favor of the LORD your God, and pray for me, that my hand may be restored to me.' And the man of God entreated the LORD, and the king's hand was restored to him and became as it was before" (1 Kings 13:6).

Jeroboam asked the man of God to come home with him so he could give him a reward along with some food and rest. The man of God told the king: "If you give me half your house, I will not go in with you. And I will not eat bread or drink water in this place, for so was it commanded me by the word of the LORD, saying, 'You shall neither eat bread nor drink water nor return by the way that you came." So he went another way and did not return by the way that he came to Bethel" (vv.8-10). The man of God from Judah was given a message to speak. He obeyed God and left.

There was an old prophet during this time that lived in Bethel. His sons came to him and told him what the man of God had done and said in Bethel. So the old prophet asked which way the man of God had gone, and he saddled a donkey and went after him. The old prophet found the man of God sitting under an oak tree and asked him if he was the man of God from Judah. The man of God told the old prophet that he was. The old prophet invited the man of God to come home with him and have something to eat. The man of God said, "I may not return with you, or go in with you, neither will I eat bread nor drink water with you in this place, for it was said to me by the word of the LORD, 'You shall neither eat bread nor drink water there, nor return by the way that you came" (1 Kings 13:16-17).

This is where the story takes a turn for the worse. The old prophet lied to the man of God by telling him that God had told him: "Bring him back with you into your house that he may eat bread and drink water" (v.18). For some reason the man of God believed the old prophet's lie even though it contradicted what God had told him. He went back with the prophet to his house. As they were sitting at the table eating, God spoke through the old prophet to give the man of God a message, since the man of God was listening to the prophet instead of Him. "And he cried to the man of God who came from Judah, 'Thus says the LORD, "Because you have disobeyed the word of the LORD and have not kept the command that the LORD your God commanded you, but have come back and have eaten bread and drunk water in the place of which he said to you, 'Eat no bread and drink no water,' your body shall not come to the tomb of your fathers"(1 Kings 13:21-22 ESV).

After the man of God had finished eating and drinking, the old prophet saddled the donkey for him so he could leave. Soon after the man of God had left, a lion met him on the road and killed him. His body was found by some men passing by. These men came into the city where the old prophet lived and told the people. When the old prophet heard it, he said, "It is the man of God who disobeyed the word of the LORD; therefore the LORD has given him to the lion, which has torn him and killed him, according to the word that the LORD spoke to him" (v.26). The old prophet went and found the body of the disobedient prophet and brought him back to be buried. The old prophet buried the disobedient prophet in his own tomb and told his sons: "When I die, bury me in the grave in which the man of God is buried; lay my bones beside his bones. For the saying that he called out by the word of the LORD against the altar in Bethel and against all the houses of the high places that are in the cities of Samaria shall surely come to pass" (vv.31-32 ESV).

When we read this story, it causes us to think and ask: "Why did the man of God listen to the old prophet and divert from God's plan?" He was very clear on what God had told him, he even repeated what God had said to him to Jeroboam and the old prophet, yet he still disobeyed. Why would he listen to a man who claimed to be a prophet if he was telling him to do the direct opposite of what God had told him? Did he disobey just on the fact that the old man said he was a prophet? Why did the man of God quickly change his mind and eat at the old prophet's house just because the old prophet said the Lord had told him he could?

If this old prophet were truly a prophet from God, he would have condemned the altar himself. Instead, God had to send a prophet all the way from Judah to cry out against it. If this old prophet were from God, he would not have lied and diverted the man of God from obeying the Lord. The old prophet succeeded in lessening the message the man of God proclaimed against Jeroboam and his altar. How did he lessen it? He caused the man of God to disobey the Lord, which resulted in him being killed by a lion. So what it actually did was strengthen those that were in rebellion by saying, "See what happened to the man of God from Judah who cried against the altar."

> *After this thing Jeroboam did not turn from his evil way, but made priests for the high places again from among all the people. Any who would, he ordained to be priests of the high places. And this thing became sin to the house of Jeroboam, so as to cut it off and to destroy it from the face of the earth.*
>
> —1 Kings 13:33-34 (ESV)

Every one of the words that the man of God spoke against Jeroboam and the altar eventually came to pass, because the words were from God. In this true biblical story, we only get to see what happens after the man of God disobeys, we don't get to see what would have happened if he had obeyed all the way through. From the moment the man of God began to listen to the false prophet, he stopped hearing from the Lord. Even the judgment that came down from God because of his disobedience had to come through the false prophet. The false prophet lied, deceived, and helped cause the man of God's death. The false prophet covered up his evil intent by acting as if he sincerely cared by burying him in his tomb and asking to be buried with him when he died. The false prophet knew that the message the man of God gave was true, that is why he wanted to lead the man of God to disobey the Lord so he could destroy his work and still come out looking like he was a prophet from God.

Instead of persevering and completing what God had told him to do, the man of God heard what he wanted to hear when the false prophet offered him food. God's plan was causing him some physical discomfort, and God was not giving him the relief he wanted. He was obviously very hungry and tired and wanted any excuse to divert from God's plan. God's plan was that he could only eat and drink when he got home. So when he heard the false prophet's message, it was what he wanted to hear.

Reading this story and knowing the outcome, we naturally ask ourselves why he disobeyed. Why did he do it? But the real question is: "Why do we do it?" Why are we so willing to disobey God's Word to satisfy our fleshly desires? Why are we willing to listen to people who tell us what we want to hear in order to satisfy our flesh and encourage complacency. Why are we so willing to justify sin and complacency in our lives? Why are we so quick to disregard or water down God's Word?

The answer is: It will cause us some discomfort or hardship if we obey God. Instead of doing God's will, we would rather follow our own will. We don't want to be inconvenienced in any way from our own plans. Consequently, we never see the fruit of an obedient life. We live our lives for the temporal pleasures of this life and never experience the joys of a faith that moves mountains—a faith that can heal, restore, and change people's lives. The Bible is very clear. It tells us how we are to live and warns us how not to live. Yet, like the disobedient prophet, many Christians do not like the answers that the Bible gives to a particular problem. So they find friends and seek council from those who tell them what they want to hear. They even find so-called spiritual people that will agree with them and appease them in their sin and rebellion, instead of giving them the truth of God's Word.

It doesn't help that there are so many ministers that are like the old prophet, they sound very spiritual and loving but will not provoke you to a holy life. The reason being that they are living in compromise and sin themselves and have never seen the fruit of obedience. They want to exercise authority over you by their position in order to steer you to their will, not God's. Their intent is for you to be dependent on their ministry instead of being dependent on God. They do not want you to hear from the Lord yourself, so you won't live a life that would convict them and show that you can live a life of love and obedience to the Lord. They are filled with pride and want to be exalted over you by having your admiration and loyalty. They do that by telling you what you want to hear. They will go out of their way to show you how loving and giving they are by being soft on sin and giving you an easy way out; they will even justify the sin in your life for you.

But it is all a smoke screen, for a true man of God will provoke you to righteousness and will never appease you in your sin. A true person of God will be merciful by pointing you to Christ so that you will repent and turn away from the bondage you're in. They do that so you can have a more obedient and closer walk with the Lord Jesus Christ. A true man of God does not want you to be stagnant and living a life of compromise. He speaks the truth out of obedience to the Lord, like the man of God did to Jeroboam. That is why the man of God cried out against Jeroboam's pagan altar—so the people would repent and worship the one true God. He showed more love by rebuking them of their idolatry than the old prophet showed by burying the man of God in his own tomb. Why? The man of God would not be dead if the old prophet had not lied to him.

We need to make sure we understand what true sincerity and love really is. Any person or minister who agrees with any attitude or lifestyle that is clearly forbidden in God's Word is not showing love or sincerity. They are definitely not showing understanding. What they are actually doing is justifying sin, for which Jesus died on the cross. Jesus spoke against sin and the need to repent all throughout the New Testament, so much so that anyone who appeases or justifies sin does not believe in the Bible. Nor do they believe in the transforming power of the Holy Spirit. Those ministers who believe this way have a religion that is driven by their flesh. Their solutions for people's problems are analyzed and worked out through human reason and ingenuity, not through biblical truth. So we never see true faith and the transforming power of the Holy Spirit in their lives.

People who serve under these ministers are led more by their feelings and emotions than by biblical truth. The only messages that they believe are from the Lord are those that make them feel good. They never learn to "walk by faith, not by sight" (2 Corinthians 5:7).

We need to obey God's Word no matter what everyone else is doing, what society is saying and how fellow Christians are living.

Like the man of God, we won't go all the way when:

1. We don't make a clean break from the past.
2. We don't get rid of compromise in our lives.
3. We don't get rid of blatant sin in our lives.
4. We don't resist and fight to overcome temptation.
5. We question God's Word.
6. We disagree with God's Word.
7. We deviate from what God has commanded.
8. We don't persevere till the end.
9. We don't obey Him no matter what.
10. We allow our feelings and human reasoning to get in the way of our obedience.

God is drawing and leading every one of us personally on a special and unique path. He has given us His Word to guide our steps and to live by. But most of the time we are willing to succumb to our fleshly desires or to listen and take direction from those who would feed that rebellion. It doesn't matter what someone else is doing, even if he is a so-called spokesman for God. If he is telling us something that is contrary to what God is telling us in His Word, we must not follow it!

Know ye not, that to whom ye yield yourselves servants to obey, his servants ye are to whom you obey; whether of sin unto death, or obedience unto righteousness?

—Romans 6:16

We are either yielding to the Holy Spirit's direction, or we're not. The Holy Spirit directs us by and through the Word of God. As we obey and follow God's Word, we are directed by Him. The more we obey the truth of God's Word, the more truth will be revealed to us. This truth will propel us to draw closer to Jesus Christ and to hunger for more of Him. It will also propel us to get rid of those things in our lives that hinder us from drawing closer to Him. So we won't be as easily led astray.

If we are not embracing God's truth, then we are yielding to our own sinful carnal nature. If we are not seeking the Lord, then we will not be convicted by the truth of God's Word. So we will start to accept what society and our carnal nature says is okay. This is sin that leads to spiritual death and separation from God. Ultimately, when we reject Jesus Christ and yield to the spirit of the world, this leads to eternal damnation in hell.

"And the world passeth away, and the lust thereof: but he that doeth the will of God abideth forever" (1 John 2:17). Just as a lion killed the man of God for his disobedience, disobedience in our lives causes the worst kind of death, a spiritual death that causes us to be comfortable in compromising and disobeying God. This attitude causes separation from God and His direction.

When the boys grew up, Esau was a skillful hunter, a man of the field, while Jacob was a quiet man, dwelling in tents. Isaac loved Esau because he ate of his game, but Rebekah loved Jacob. Once when Jacob was cooking stew, Esau came in from the field, and he was exhausted. And Esau said to Jacob, "Let me eat some of that red stew, for I am exhausted!" (Therefore his name was called Edom.) Jacob said, "Sell me your birthright now." Esau said, "I am about to die; of what use is a birthright to me?" Jacob said, "Swear to me now." So he swore to him and sold his birthright to Jacob. Then

*Jacob gave Esau bread and lentil stew, and he ate and drank and
rose and went his way. Thus Esau despised his birthright.*

—Genesis 25:27-34 (ESV)

The birthright that Jacob wanted and Esau didn't care about was a special blessing given to the firstborn son. Because Esau was the firstborn son, he would receive the spiritual and material blessing passed down from his father Isaac. The firstborn had the privilege of ruling over their families just on the fact of their birthright. Jacob was obviously thinking about the birthright and wanted it. He knew how important the birthright was and wanted the spiritual blessing it brought.

Jacob was cooking some red stew when Esau came back from the field. Esau was very hungry and exhausted and asked Jacob for some of his stew. Jacob said he would give Esau some food if he sold him his birthright. Esau, who was only thinking about his temporal needs, said, "I am about to die; of what use is a birthright to me?" So Jacob had his brother swear to him that he would sell his birthright for some food. Esau did swear to Jacob and was given some food, and when he was done eating he left. Esau did not try to recant what he had said or accuse Jacob of coercing him. He left, not thinking anymore about it. That is why Genesis 25:34 says: "Thus Esau despised his birthright."

Esau easily sold his birthright for some food from Jacob, for he was only thinking about his fleshly needs. He was only living for the moment and not the future. He was hungry, and all he cared about was satisfying that craving. Obviously his birthright did not mean that much to him. When we are born again, we are adopted into God's family and become His children. We must protect our birthright!

*But to all who did receive him, who believed in his name, he gave
the right to become children of God, who were born, not of blood nor
of the will of the flesh nor of the will of man, but of God.*

—John 1:12-13 (ESV)

For ye are all the children of God by faith in Christ Jesus.

—Galatians 3:26

We must protect our birthright at all costs! We have been given so many promises in the Word that are there for the asking. We must persevere and wait for them to come to pass. Our relationship with Jesus Christ is the most important thing we have. If we start taking our relationship for granted by not pursuing a deeper, more obedient faith, then we allow all kinds of hurtful attitudes and hindrances in our walk with the Lord. This prevents us from obtaining those promises the Bible has given us. When we disregard the warnings in the Bible and disobey what God is telling us, we ruin our lives and it becomes harder to get back to where we should be. Disobedience starts from not taking our birthright seriously and only thinking about our temporal needs—satisfying our flesh. Obedience is not easy, for it requires perseverance, and we will experience hardship because of it. We will be inconvenienced and experience all kinds of physical and spiritual challenges in the process of living an obedient life. The reality is that the joy of obtaining the prize outweighs any kind of earthly temporal pleasure or hardship. Those who hunger and thirst for more of Jesus Christ absolutely know that to be true!

Esau despised and lost his birthright to his younger brother Jacob because it meant nothing to him. Esau never showed any kind of regret for what he did; he only cared about satisfying his flesh. He never repented from taking his birthright for granted. He only blamed Jacob for his part. Esau only cared about the birthright when his father was dying because he wanted the material part of the blessing. This is typical for those who say they love Jesus Christ but never progress in their faith, or who never overcome the bondage in their lives that keeps them stagnant and impotent. They want the blessings of the Bible without having to persevere. They're in bondage to the same sin year after year, and it's ruining their lives. Their excuse is always a fleshly excuse and someone else's fault. They are unwilling to fight, persevere, and run hard after Jesus Christ for the grace to overcome sin. Esau lost his birthright because he took it for granted.

No servant can serve two masters: for either he will hate the one, and love the other; or else he will hold to the one, and despise the other. Ye cannot serve God and mammon.

—Luke 16:13

As Christians, we cannot serve two masters. Either we will serve the one and despise the other, or we will love the one and hate the other. If we love God, we will naturally despise the things of the world that are contrary to God. If we love the sinful pleasures of this world, we will despise His commands. "Ye cannot serve God and mammon." You cannot serve God and riches or any other thing you trust and rely on more than God. We cannot serve both! If we are truly serving the Lord, we will not want to take part in those things that will hinder us from serving Him.

We see so many people trying to be a servant to both. They live in the middle ground, living for the temporal pleasures of this world and trying to serve Christ. They don't want to go too far into the sinfulness of the society around them, but they don't want to forsake it either. They don't want to go all the way with Christ, because it demands forsaking the sinfulness of the world. It demands separation. The people who live in this compromised state are not happy serving either, because they have a divided heart. Some days they're one way, and some days they're the other way. What group they're in will determine how they will be. They never experience the joys and pleasure of living an obedient, faithful life. They are easily led astray by lukewarm Christians who try to divert them from actually living for Jesus Christ, like what happened to the man of God. Or they easily compromise their faith for the temporal pleasures of satisfying their flesh as Esau did.

> *And he said to them all, if any man will come after me, let him deny himself, and take up his cross daily, and follow me. For whosoever will save his life shall lose it: but whosoever will lose his life for my sake, the same shall save it. For what is a man advantaged, if he gain the whole world, and lose himself, or be cast away? For whosoever shall be ashamed of me and of my words, of him shall the Son of man be ashamed, when he shall come in his own glory, and in his Father's, and of the holy angels.*
>
> —Luke 9:23-26

CHAPTER 4

▼

THE OPPOSITE OF FEAR
IS FAITH

Nebuchadnezzar answered and said to them, "Is it true, O Shadrach, Meshach, and Abednego, that you do not serve my gods or worship the golden image that I have set up? Now if you are ready when you hear the sound of the horn, pipe, lyre, trigon, harp, bagpipe, and every kind of music, to fall down and worship the image that I have made, well and good. But if you do not worship, you shall immediately be cast into a burning fiery furnace. And who is the god who will deliver you out of my hands?" Shadrach, Meshach, and Abednego answered and said to the king, "O Nebuchadnezzar, we have no need to answer you in this matter. If this be so, our God whom we serve is able to deliver us from the burning fiery furnace, and he will deliver us out of your hand, O king. But if not, be it known to you, O king, that we will not serve your gods or worship the golden image that you have set up." Then Nebuchadnezzar was filled with fury, and the expression of his face was changed against Shadrach, Meshach, and Abednego. He ordered the furnace heated seven times more than it was usually heated. And he ordered some of the mighty men of his army to bind Shadrach, Meshach, and Abednego, and to cast them into the burning fiery furnace. Then these

men were bound in their cloaks, their tunics, their hats, and their
other garments, and they were thrown into the burning fiery furnace.
—Daniel 3:14-21 (ESV)

The book of Daniel describes what happened to Daniel and the Jews during their captivity in Babylon. The book of Daniel is a prophetic book with visions and prophecies, which foretell important events that relate to the four great empires of the world. It also foretells the coming Messiah and His death, the Gentiles being converted, and the Jews being restored.

When we look at this book, we must keep in mind that Daniel, who was from the family of Judah, was a captive carried away to Babylon as a youth. He went to Babylon, a city far away from Jerusalem, which not only had different customs but also had a different language. Daniel and his friends were Jews in a land that did not recognize their religion. The people in the land were pagans with many idols. In this chapter, we are going to study Daniel and his friends' uncompromising loyalty to God, in the midst of idolatry and in the face of death.

Jehoiakim was king of Judah when Nebuchadnezzar king of Babylon came to Jerusalem and took it. The king commanded his chief eunuch to bring some of the captives from Israel who were descended from royalty. He wanted "youths without blemish, of good appearance and skillful in all wisdom, endowed with knowledge, understanding learning, and competent to stand in the king's palace, and to teach them the literature and language of the Chaldeans" (Dan. 1:4). These youths were to be given a daily portion of food and wine from the king's table. They were also to be educated for three years before they were allowed to stand before the king. Among these youths were Daniel, Hananiah, Mishael, and Azariah of the tribe of Judah.

When they arrived in Babylon, their captors changed their Hebrew names to try to get them to forget the God of their fathers. Daniel was changed to Belteshazzar, Hananiah to Shadrach, Mishael to Meshach, and Azariah to Abednego. They were named after the pagan gods that the people in Babylon worshiped. Their whole lives were changed to reflect the heathen society around them. But no matter how hard they tried to change them, they remained loyal to the God of their fathers.

Daniel resolved not to defile himself with the king's food or wine, because the king's food was offered up to idols to honor them. Most likely, the food was also in question because the Jews had strict dietary restrictions. God's Word forbid sacrificing to idols—to participate in eating the king's food would be compromising the faith and condoning idolatry. So Daniel asked the chief of the eunuchs to allow him not to defile himself with the king's food but be given different food. God had given favor to Daniel in the sight of the chief of the eunuchs. But the chief of the eunuchs said, "I fear my lord the king, who assigned your food and your drink; for why should he see that you were in worse condition than the youths who are of your own age? So you would endanger my head with the king" (Dan. 1:10). The chief of the eunuchs was worried that if he allowed Daniel and his friends to eat food other than what the king was providing, they would physically look worse than the other youths. If, after three years, Daniel and his three friends looked worse than the others, the chief of the eunuchs would be in serious trouble for not making them eat the king's food.

Daniel pressed the issue and asked the steward who was assigned over them: "Test your servants for ten days; let us be given vegetables to eat and water to drink. Then let our appearance and the appearance of the youths who eat the king's food be observed by you, and deal with your servants according to what you see" (Dan. 1:12-13). The steward listened to them and tested them for ten days. God honored Daniel, Shadrach, Meshach, and Abednego for their obedience. After ten days, their appearance was better than that of the youths who ate the king's food. So the steward no longer required them to eat the food and wine from the king's table and gave them the food they requested instead.

As for these four youths, God gave them learning and skill in all literature and wisdom, and Daniel had understanding in all visions and dreams. At the end of the time, when the king had commanded that they should be brought in, the chief of the eunuchs brought them in before Nebuchadnezzar. And the king spoke with them, and among all of them none was found like Daniel, Hananiah, Mishael, and Azariah. Therefore they stood before the king. And in every matter of wisdom and understanding about which the king inquired of them, he found them ten times better than all the magicians and enchanters that were in all his kingdom. And Daniel was there until the first year of King Cyrus.

—Daniel 1:17-21 (ESV)

God gave Daniel great wisdom and understanding and the ability to interpret dreams. Daniel soon gained great favor with King Nebuchadnezzar because he interpreted a dream for him. The king was so grateful for the interpretation that he fell on his face and "paid homage to Daniel" and commanded that they make an offering and offer up incense to him. The king said to Daniel, "Truly, your God is God of gods and Lord of kings, and a revealer of mysteries, for you have been able to reveal this mystery" (Dan. 2:47). The king honored Daniel with gifts and made him ruler over the province of Babylon and the chief prefect over all the wise men in Babylon. Daniel requested from the king that he appoint Shadrach, Meshach, and Abednego over the affairs of the province of Babylon. The king granted Daniel his request, and Daniel remained in the king's court.

King Nebuchadnezzar made a statue of gold that was 90 feet high[1] and set it up in the province of Babylon. Then King Nebuchadnezzar gathered all the head officials and governors to come to the dedication of the statue he had set up. When all the people were gathered together for the dedication, King Nebuchadnezzar had a herald proclaim, "You are commanded, O peoples, nations, and languages, that when you hear the sound of the horn, pipe, lyre, trigon, harp, bagpipe, and every kind of music, you are to fall down and worship the golden image that King Nebuchadnezzar has set up. And whoever does not fall down and worship shall immediately be cast into a burning fiery furnace.' Therefore, as soon as all the peoples heard the sound of the horn, pipe, lyre, trigon, harp, bagpipe, and every kind of music, all the peoples, nations, and languages fell down and worshiped the golden image that King Nebuchadnezzar had set up" (Dan. 3:4-7 ESV).

Some Chaldeans came forward to maliciously tell King Nebuchadnezzar that certain Jews he had appointed over the affairs of the province of Babylon were not falling down to worship the image when the music was played. They reminded the king that he had made a decree that if anyone did not bow down to the image when the music was played, that person would be cast into the fiery furnace. They told the king that Shadrach, Meshach, and Abednego were disregarding his decree. When Nebuchadnezzar heard this, he was very angry and had them brought to him. Nebuchadnezzar said to them: "Is it true, O Shadrach, Meshach, and Abednego, that you do not serve my gods or worship the golden image that I have set up?" (v.14).

The king told them if they fell down and worshiped the image when they heard the music, they would not be punished, but if they didn't, they would immediately be thrown into the fiery furnace, and concluded by saying: "And who is the god who will deliver you out of my hands?" (v.15). Shadrach, Meshach, and Abednego told the king they didn't even have to think about the matter. They told him that the God they serve was able to deliver them from the burning fiery furnace, but that even if God did not deliver them, they would "not serve your gods or worship the golden image that you have set up" (v.18). Nebuchadnezzar got really angry and ordered the furnace to be "heated seven times more than it was usually heated" (v.19). So the soldiers bound Shadrach, Meshach, and Abednego and threw them into the furnace. The fire was so hot that the flames killed the soldiers who threw them in the oven.

Shadrach, Meshach, and Abednego landed in the burning fiery furnace bound in their clothes. As King Nebuchadnezzar was watching, he rose up and asked his counselors: "Did we not cast three men bound into the fire?" (v.24). His counselors told the king that they had. The King said, "But I see four men unbound, walking in the midst of the fire, and they are not hurt; and the appearance of the fourth is like a son of the gods" (v.25). Then Nebuchadnezzar called out: "Shadrach, Meshach, and Abednego, servants of the Most High God, come out, and come here!" (v.26). Then the three came out of the fire. Everyone who was there that day and had watched Shadrach, Meshach, and Abednego get thrown into the fire, were amazed because the fire did not affect them at all. The hair on their heads was not singed nor were their clothes burned up. They didn't even smell like smoke!

Nebuchadnezzar answered and said, "Blessed be the God of Shadrach, Meshach, and Abednego, who has sent his angel and delivered his servants, who trusted in him, and set aside the king's command, and yielded up their bodies rather than serve and worship any god except their own God. Therefore I make a decree: Any people, nation, or language that speaks anything against the God of Shadrach, Meshach, and Abednego shall be torn limb from limb, and their houses laid in ruins, for there is no other god who is able to rescue in this way." Then the king promoted Shadrach, Meshach, and Abednego in the province of Babylon.

—Daniel 3:28-30 (ESV)

The king said, "But I see four men unbound, walking in the midst of the fire, and they are not hurt; and the appearance of the fourth is like a son of the gods" (v.25). During this fiery trial, the Son of God, the pre-incarnate Christ, was with them. God's presence was physically there to get them through. The Bible gives us many promises of His abiding presence in our lives and His utter faithfulness during our trials. Just to name a few of His promises:

1. "I will never leave thee, nor forsake thee" (Heb. 13:5).

2. "Be strong and of a good courage, fear not, nor be afraid of them: for the Lord thy God, he it is that doth go with thee; he will not fail thee; nor forsake thee" (Deut. 31:6).

3. "Lo, I am with you always, even unto the end of the world" (Matt. 28:20).

4. "When thou walkest through the fire, thou shalt not be burned; neither shall the flame kindle upon thee" (Isa. 43:2).

Shadrach, Meshach, and Abednego told the king they would not bow down to the image and worship it. No matter what the king had done to them, they would not have bowed down to the image. They were confident that God was able to deliver them from the fiery furnace, and even if He didn't deliver them, they were not going to compromise their faith. Even if it was God's will that they die in the fiery furnace, they were ready to submit to His will and honor Him. They knew that the outcome of their obedience would glorify God. Shadrach, Meshach, and Abednego's obedience had such an impact on the king because, as he said, they "set aside the king's command, and yielded up their bodies rather than serve and worship any god except their own God" (v.28). They were so mightily delivered that the king made a decree: "Any people, nation, or language that speaks anything against the God of Shadrach, Meshach, and Abednego shall be torn limb from limb, and their houses laid in ruins, for there is no other god who is able to rescue in this way" (v.29). Then the king promoted them.

Daniel, Shadrach, Meshach, and Abednego were faithful to God in everything they did, and the Lord gave them favor with whomever they served. They served several kings in their lifetime of captivity and were faithful to God throughout. During the reign of Darius, Daniel was very old and yet he still held a high position with the king. There were three presidents that ruled over 120 satraps (princes) that ruled over the kingdom, and Daniel was one of the three.

Daniel had distinguished himself above all the other presidents and satraps, "because an excellent spirit was in him" (Dan. 6:3). The king's plan was to set Daniel over the whole kingdom.

> *Then the presidents and the satraps sought to find a ground for complaint against Daniel with regard to the kingdom, but they could find no ground for complaint or any fault, because he was faithful, and no error or fault was found in him. Then these men said, "We shall not find any ground for complaint against this Daniel unless we find it in connection with the law of his God."*
>
> —Daniel 6:4-5 (ESV)

These other presidents and satraps were jealous of Daniel and tried to find a reason to accuse him of some misdeed before the king. But there was nothing they could accuse him of other than finding something in connection to his faith in God. So they came together, wrote up a document, and brought it to the king saying, "that whoever makes petition to any god or man for thirty days, except to you, O king, shall be cast into the den of lions" (v.7). The king signed the document and established the law. The law the king established could never be revoked, according to the law of the Medes and the Persians.

Even though Daniel knew that this document had been signed, he did not cease from praying to the Lord. As a matter of fact, he did not even try to hide his praying. Three times a day he went to the upper chamber of his house and prayed on his knees with the window open toward Jerusalem.

When some men saw Daniel violating the law by praying, they came before the king to remind him of the law he had signed. They did this because they knew the king loved Daniel. So they asked him: "Did you not sign an injunction, that anyone who makes petition to any god or man within thirty days except to you, O king, shall be cast into the den of lions?" (v.12). The king said that he had signed the law and it couldn't be revoked. Then they told the king that Daniel was ignoring the law by praying three times a day.

"Then the king, when he heard these words, was much distressed and set his mind to deliver Daniel. And he labored till the sun went down to rescue him. Then these men came by agreement to the king and said to the king, 'Know, O king, that it is a law of the Medes and Persians that no injunction or ordinance that the king establishes can be changed.' Then the king commanded, and Daniel was brought and cast into the den of lions. The king declared to Daniel, 'May your God, whom you serve continually, deliver you!'" (Dan. 6:14-16 ESV).

The king did not want to throw Daniel into the lions' den. He was distressed by the decision and "labored till the sun went down to rescue him" (v.14). But those who accused Daniel reminded the king that the law of the Medes and Persians could not be changed. The king succumbed to their pressure and commanded that Daniel be thrown into the lions' den. After Daniel was thrown in, a stone was laid on the opening of the den and the king sealed it with his own signet. Daniel was loyal to the king and served him faithfully. Now the king whom he faithfully served was throwing him into the lions' den. Daniel did not get angry at the king or try to defend himself by pointing out all that he had done for him. Daniel did not look at the situation that way. His confidence and trust was in God, not man. He looked only to God for deliverance and was confident He would deliver.

The king spent the whole night fasting. His conscience bothered him so much that he could not sleep. Like anyone who has made a rash decision only to wish they had never made that decision, he was restless. He was probably wishing he had not been influenced by the men who had acted like they were trying to honor him but had instead used him to destroy Daniel. Now the king was hoping that Daniel would be delivered by his God so that his regretful decision could be turned around.

> *Then, at break of day, the king arose and went in haste to the den of lions. As he came near to the den where Daniel was, he cried out in a tone of anguish. The king declared to Daniel, "O Daniel, servant of the living God, has your God, whom you serve continually, been able to deliver you from the lions?" Then Daniel said to the king, "O king, live forever! My God sent his angel and shut the lions' mouths, and they have not harmed me, because I was found blameless before him; and also before you, O king, I have done no harm."*
>
> —Daniel 6:19-22 (ESV)

The king could not wait to see if God had delivered Daniel and was "exceedingly glad" when he found out He had. He immediately ordered Daniel to be taken out of the lions' den. Daniel was not harmed in any way because he trusted in God, and God had protected him. The king commanded that the men who had maliciously accused Daniel be thrown into the lions' den along with their wives and children. Before they hit the bottom of the den, they were torn apart and killed by the lions. Their fate is exactly the same as those who try to destroy and hinder people's faith; they destroy themselves and their families in the process. The king made a decree "'that in all my royal dominion people are to tremble and fear before the God of Daniel, for he is the living God, enduring forever; his kingdom shall never be destroyed, and his dominion shall be to the end. He delivers and rescues; he works signs and wonders in heaven and on earth, he who has saved Daniel from the power of the lions.' So this Daniel prospered during the reign of Darius and the reign of Cyrus the Persian" (Dan. 6:26-28 ESV).

Daniel, Shadrach, Meshach, and Abednego would not compromise their faith no matter what the circumstances. Starting at a young age, they determined not to be pressured or influenced by fear to disobey the Lord. They obeyed the Lord in the simplest matters, which prepared them for the bigger tests of faith. They spent their lives in captivity away from their families. They lived in a foreign land that was full of idolatry, yet they determined not to defile themselves with the evil influences around them. They did not use their circumstances or conditions as an excuse not to serve the Lord.

They did not allow themselves to be ruled by fear. Fear leads to unsound decisions, compromise, and disobedience. A life of self-preservation, instead of self-denial, will lead to an unhealthy focus on temporal comfort and security. They influenced kings and kingdoms through their obedience. In the face of death, they did not back down from their faith in God. Ultimately, every king they served publicly admitted that Daniel, Shadrach, Meshach, and Abednego's God was the one true God, and they honored them. God gave them favor and promoted them to the highest positions in the kingdom. They overcame fear by their strong faith in God, and they obtained this faith by knowing God. They spent a lifetime seeking and following God. Therefore they knew how faithful He was. For He said, "I will never leave thee, nor forsake thee" (Heb. 13:5).

Studying the book of Daniel, we all should be convicted by the fact that they were not willing to compromise their faith, no matter what. If most of us took an honest look at our faith, we would see how easily we allow fear to influence and cause us to compromise and disobey. If you look at most Christians, their decisions are based on unfounded fears: choosing security and not taking a stand in the face of evil.

We know we are influenced more by fear than by faith when:

1. We are afraid to witness because we don't want to look bad or it embarrasses us or we are afraid it will alienate us from the group.

2. We are afraid to make a moral stand in our workplace, school, community, and with our friends because it might cause us hardship.

3. We are more concerned about our temporal comfort than about someone else's eternal state.

4. We are more concerned with fitting in or being liked than obeying the Lord.

5. We are more concerned about job security than fulfilling God's will.

6. We are more concerned about losing our jobs than glorifying God.

7. Our security is in the temporal things of this life such as money, retirement, insurance, family, health, and institutions other than in the promises of God—when our life revolves around these things and not around Jesus Christ and fulfilling His will.

If what happened to Daniel, Shadrach, Meshach, and Abednego happened today in America, what kind of advice would they receive from fellow Christians? Would we tell them to bow down to the idols so they would not get thrown into the oven? Would we tell them more good would come out of the situation by "staying alive" than by being martyred for the faith? Would we tell them to take the easy way out by justifying their disobedience in the situation? No matter what the circumstances, nothing good will come out of disobeying the Lord. Avoiding a trial or a test out of fear is avoiding the opportunity for God to use you to glorify Him. What if Daniel and his friends had succumbed to the fear of dying and had bowed down to the idols instead? How would that have glorified God? Even if they had been killed, their obedience would have glorified God more than if they had compromised their faith. If they had bowed down to idols, the kings would have seen that they were not that adamant about following their God. They would have seen that they truly didn't trust God. Ultimately, the kings would have thought that Daniel and his friends' God must not be real, because they were unwilling to take a stand for Him.

God works powerfully in the lives of people who have settled in their heart that they will not compromise their faith no matter what. The world is watching those of us who profess to have faith in Jesus Christ. They are watching how we react and how adamant we are about living for Him. To have the kind of faith that Daniel and his friends had does not happen overnight or does not result from one's own strength. It happens when we obey the Lord in the most basic things and won't compromise in the very least of things. Over time, as we are tested in a greater measure, it becomes easier to obey the greater things because we have lived an uncompromising obedient life in the little things.

As we get closer to the Lord and our faith grows, we naturally will live a life of self-denial and will see things through the eyes of faith, or see things in the light of eternity. Then we are less likely to allow fear to ruin our faith and growth in Him. We can't say that we would die for Him physically, if we are unwilling to die for Him in the very least of things like our reputation, our job, with our friends, or by taking a stand against immorality.

And I say unto you my friends, Be not afraid of them that kill the body, and after that have no more that they can do. But I will forewarn you whom ye shall fear: Fear him, which after he hath killed hath power to cast into hell; yea, I say unto you, Fear him.

—Luke 12:4-5

So that we may boldly say, The Lord is my helper, and I will not fear what man shall do unto me.

—Hebrews 13:6

If we truly love Jesus Christ, then we will naturally obey Him in all aspects of our lives. We will not want to participate in or do anything that would hinder our relationship with Him. We won't want to do anything that will misrepresent Him or demean Him in any way. We will have a natural fear to protect our relationship with Him. We will have reverence for and take serious the promises and judgments in His Word. Just as in a relationship with another person, whether it is a wife or husband or other loved one, we will fear to betray that person or participate in certain things because we don't want to injure or ruin our relationship.

The fear we are to have for God is a healthy fear. The more we fear God, the less we will fear man. Man can't give eternal life or stop someone from obtaining it. It is only through the righteousness of Jesus Christ that we have eternal life. It does not matter how admired we are in this world, if we reject Jesus Christ we will suffer the wrath of God and eternity in hell. The most man could ever do to us is kill our temporal body—we would still live eternally with Christ.

If we have an intimate relationship with Jesus Christ, we need to do whatever it takes to protect that relationship. We will not want to compromise that relationship no matter what the circumstances might be. Just as we learned from Daniel, Shadrach, Meshach, and Abednego, no circumstance we might find ourselves in will ever become an excuse not to wholeheartedly serve the Lord. We should fear disobeying Him and allowing anything to get in the way of that relationship. We should live our lives to please Him and not man—no matter what!

> *Trust in the LORD with all thine heart; and lean not unto thine own understanding. In all thy ways acknowledge him, and he shall direct thy paths. Be not wise in thine own eyes: fear the LORD, and depart from evil.*
>
> —Proverbs 3:5-7

CHAPTER 5

▼

THEY HAVE NOT KNOWN
MY WAYS

Wherefore (as the Holy Ghost saith, To day if ye will hear his voice, harden not your hearts, as in the provocation, in the day of temptation in the wilderness: When your fathers tempted me, proved me, and saw my works forty years. Wherefore I was grieved with that generation, and said, They do alway err in their heart; and they have not known my ways. So I sware in my wrath, They shall not enter into my rest.) Take heed, brethren, lest there be in any of you an evil heart of unbelief, in departing from the living God. But exhort one another daily, while it is called To day; lest any of you be hardened through the deceitfulness of sin.

—Hebrews 3:7-13

A year after God had delivered the children of Israel out of Egypt, they arrived at the Promised Land (Canaan). God had promised the land of Canaan to the Israelites, which is how it got its name, the Promised Land. When they arrived at the edge of the Promised Land, Moses said, "Go up, take possession, as the LORD, the God of your fathers, has told you. Do not fear or be dismayed" (Deut. 1:21 ESV). Instead of the people going right in to take the Promised Land, they came to Moses and asked him to send men to explore the land first. Instead of consulting with the Lord before answering the people's request, Moses said, "The thing seemed good to me" (v.23), and chose 12 men, one from every tribe, to spy out the land. Sending out the 12 men to spy out the land turned out to be a grave error.

God allowed the children of Israel to send out 12 spies in order to test and try them. God told Moses to send the men to spy out the land according to their desire, so they could see the land He was giving them (Num. 13:1-2). Moses told the 12 men: "See what the land is, and whether the people who dwell in it are strong or weak, whether they are few or many, and whether the land that they dwell in is good or bad, and whether the cities that they dwell in are camps or strongholds, and whether the land is rich or poor, and whether there are trees in it or not. Be of good courage and bring some of the fruit of the land" (Num. 13:18-20 ESV).

After the spies returned from exploring the land for 40 days, Moses told them to give an account of what they found. They said that the land was very good and fruitful but that the people who lived in the land were very strong and lived within large, fortified cities. Caleb, who was one of the 12 who spied out the land, said, "Let us go up at once and occupy it, for we are well able to overcome it" (v.30). But the other men (except Joshua) who had gone with Caleb told the people that they were unable to go against the inhabitants of the land, because they were stronger than them. They spread fear and a bad report by telling the people that the land "devours its inhabitants, and all the people that we saw in it are of great height ... and we seemed to ourselves like grasshoppers, and so we seemed to them" (vv.32-33). Not only did they give a false report but they exaggerated the description of the inhabitants by saying they were like *grasshoppers* to them. They did not trust the promises that God had given them the land to possess—the promise that He would be with them as they destroyed the inhabitants of the land. They looked at the situation in the natural and spread fear and a false report among the people.

Fear spread throughout the people because they believed the false report instead of the promises of God. They began to complain and speak out against Moses and Aaron and said to them that it would have been better for them to die in Egypt or in the wilderness: "Why is the LORD bringing us into this land, to fall by the sword? Our wives and our little ones will become a prey. Would it not be better for us to go back to Egypt?" (Num. 14:3 ESV). They said to each other: "Let us choose a leader and go back to Egypt" (v.4).

Moses and Aaron fell on their faces before the people and pleaded with them not to disobey the Lord. Then Joshua and Caleb, who were part of the 12, "tore their clothes and said to all the congregation of the people of Israel, 'The land, which we passed through to spy it out, is an exceedingly good land. If the LORD delights in us, he will bring us into this land and give it to us, a land that flows with milk and honey. Only do not rebel against the LORD. And do not fear the people of the land, for they are bread for us. Their protection is removed from them, and the LORD is with us; do not fear them.' Then all the congregation said to stone them with stones" (Num. 14:6-10 ESV).

The Lord spoke to Moses, "How long will this people despise me? And how long will they not believe in me, in spite of all the signs that I have done among them? I will strike them with the pestilence and disinherit them, and I will make of you a nation greater and mightier than they" (Num. 14:11-12 ESV). The Lord was very angry with the people because they did not believe Him despite all the miracles He had done for them and how faithful He was to them. Not only had He sustained them in the wilderness, but He had delivered them from Egypt with mighty signs and wonders. He had delivered them according to their heart's cry when they were slaves in Egypt. He had parted the Red Sea so they could cross over on dry land and escape the approaching Egyptian army that hoped to destroy them. They watched as God destroyed the Egyptians by the receding waters after they were safely across the Red Sea. Despite all this, the Israelites did not believe God's promises He had made to them. They believed man's report, not God's.

God wanted to destroy the children of Israel and disinherit them because of their disobedience. He wanted to raise up for Moses another group of people that would be greater and mightier than the Israelites. But Moses interceded for the people by pleading with God not to destroy them. Moses told God that if He destroyed the children of Israel, the

Egyptians and the inhabitants of the land would hear of it and say that the Lord was unable to deliver the Israelites and bring them into the Promised Land, so He killed them in the wilderness instead. If He destroyed the Israelites, it would make Him look like He was weak and unable to fulfill His promises.

Moses pleaded with God to forgive the people as He had forgiven them so many times before. "And now, please let the power of the Lord be great as you have promised, saying, 'The LORD is slow to anger and abounding in steadfast love, forgiving iniquity and transgression, but he will by no means clear the guilty, visiting the iniquity of the fathers on the children, to the third and the fourth generation'" (Num. 14:17-18 ESV).

The Lord pardoned the people according to Moses' request and did not destroy those who disobeyed. But none of them were allowed to enter into the Promised Land, because they were unbelieving and fearful. They had experienced God's mighty deliverance and had seen His supernatural miracles—yet they did not believe He would bring them into the Promised Land. When it came time to go in and fight for the Promised Land, they were overcome by fear of man and not by faith in God's Word. None of those who despised His Word would ever see the land He promised to their Fathers. Only Joshua and Caleb would be allowed to enter into the Promised Land with a new generation.

The Lord told Moses to take the children of Israel back into the wilderness toward the Red Sea. He also told them that none of the people who grumbled against Him would enter into the Promised Land. Any person who was 20 years or older would die in the wilderness and never enter the land that He promised them, except for Joshua and Caleb. The children of those who died in the wilderness would be the ones to inherit the Promised Land. Prior to that, they must wander in the desert for 40 years because of their parents' lack of faith. They had to wander one year for every day the spies had spied out the Promised Land, which was 40 days.

God sent a plague on the 10 men who came back from spying and who spread fear among the people, and they died. Only Joshua and Caleb remained alive of those that spied out the land. They remained alive because they believed God's promises and wanted to take the land that

God had given them. When Moses told the people they would die in the wilderness and never enter the Promised Land, "the people mourned greatly."

> *And they rose early in the morning and went up to the heights of the hill country, saying, "Here we are. We will go up to the place that the LORD has promised, for we have sinned." But Moses said, "Why now are you transgressing the command of the LORD, when that will not succeed? Do not go up, for the Lord is not among you, lest you be struck down before your enemies. For there the Amalekites and the Canaanites are facing you, and you shall fall by the sword. Because you have turned back from following the LORD, the LORD will not be with you." But they presumed to go up to the heights of the hill country, although neither the ark of the covenant of the LORD nor Moses departed out of the camp. Then the Amalekites and the Canaanites who lived in that hill country came down and defeated them and pursued them, even to Hormah.*
>
> —Numbers 14:40-45

The Israelites regretted their disobedience to the Lord. When they found out what they were missing and about the punishment for not going into the Promised Land, they decided to go into the Promised Land on their own, even though the Lord had told them that they would not be able to do so. Once again the Israelites chose to disobey the Lord. They had their chance to go in when God wanted them to, but they blew that chance. So Moses pleaded with them not to disobey the Lord again.

They did not listen. They decided to go out early the next morning to take possession of the Promised Land. They failed to enter the land the day prior because of their unbelief, and now they were trying to enter in their own strength. But because God's blessing and protection were not with them, they were utterly defeated. They were destroyed by the enemy because the Lord's protection and blessing was not with them. Their unbelief led to their disobedience, which led to the consequences of their disobedience.

What was the result of their unbelief?

1. The people's fears were unfounded.

2. The people rebelled and were disobedient.

3. The Israelites lost God's protection and blessing.

4. The 10 faithless spies were killed by plague.

5. Adults 20 years and older did not obtain the Promised Land.

6. The people did not have a permanent home; they lived in tents instead.

7. The people were defeated in battle without the Lords protection and blessing.

8. For forty years the people wandered in the wilderness, reminded daily of what they could have had if they had not disobeyed.

9. Their children did not receive the blessing of growing up in the Promised Land.

10. The children shared in their parents' disobedience.

Forty years later, after the death of all those who had disobeyed God, Joshua and the new generation that grew up in the wilderness entered into the Promised Land.

> *For whatever was written in former days was written for our instruction, that through endurance and through the encouragement of the Scriptures we might have hope.*
>
> —Romans 15:4 (ESV)

The story of the Israelites' failure to enter into the Promised Land the first time is there for us to learn from. It clearly shows us the cost of not believing what the Lord says. When we do not follow and obey God's Word, we suffer the punishment of our disobedience. We also suffer by not receiving the blessings that obedience brings in our lives, which will directly affect our children's lives. As we see from the example of the Israelites, it can even cost us our physical lives. Ultimately, if we do not believe and obey God's Word, we will never obtain eternal life.

The Holy Spirit is speaking to us through their lives. When God speaks to us, we should not harden our hearts to His Word, but obey it. We should obey what the Lord is telling us no matter how things appear or what other people are saying. We can't allow unfounded, perceived, or even real fear to get in the way of God's will. If we do not obey the Lord's voice, our hearts will become hardened to it. Then we will no longer recognize His voice, and we will start working things out according to our own ways or the ways of others.

That's why in Hebrews 3:10 it says, "They do alway err in their heart; and they have not known my ways." This is what it all comes down to—they have not "known my ways." They do not know the Lord, for if they knew Him, they would obey Him. If the Israelites were seeking the Lord, as were Joshua and Caleb, they would have believed and obeyed God. They would not have believed the false and exaggerated report that caused fear and unbelief among the people. But because they truly did not know the Lord, they disobeyed Him. Their confidence was not in the Lord but in themselves and other people. They didn't have enough faith in God's Word to trust and obey Him. They could not see past their situation and other people's lies.

When God delivered the children of Israel out of Egypt, they should have entered the Promised Land one year after their deliverance. Instead, they wandered in the desert for another 39 years. During that time of wandering in the desert, a new generation learned to obey God's voice explicitly. They were able to remain a separate people, not influenced by the evil of the pagan people around them. Most of all, they were able to get rid of the "Egypt" mentality that hurt their parents. Their parents were always looking back to Egypt's security. They always wanted to go back. They always exaggerated how good the conditions were in Egypt. They never forsook the old life and embraced the new. This fact manifested itself when they were tested. They did not enter the Promised Land because of unbelief.

Joshua, who had the testimony that he was a seeker of God, led a new generation into the Promised Land. Joshua trained and learned from Moses and was given the honor of leading this new generation because of his faithfulness to the Lord. Of the 12 spies, only Joshua and Caleb believed God. They stood up against all the people exhorting them to obey God and take the Promised Land (Num. 14:6-9 ESV). They did not give up on the people but persevered in the desert to bring the new generation into the Promised Land.

The old Egypt mentality was gone and a new generation that trusted and believed God emerged. They had a different mentality—they looked forward, never looking back, to obtaining the promises of God. They wanted to obey and follow the Lord no matter what. They were so obedient that when they got to the edge of the Promised Land, they told Joshua: "All that you have commanded us we will do, and wherever you send us we will go. Just as we obeyed Moses in all things, so we will obey you. Only may the LORD your God be with you, as he was with Moses! Whoever rebels against your commandment and disobeys your words, whatever you command him, shall be put to death. Only be strong and courageous" (Joshua 1:16-18 ESV).

The first generation never entered into the Promised Land because they did not know the Lord. They were not intimate with Him. Therefore, when tested they failed because they relied on what they knew—their own feelings and perceived reality of the situation. They could not get beyond themselves and the Egyptian mentality they were comfortable with. It did not matter that they had experienced firsthand numerous supernatural miracles and seen how faithful God was. When tested, they did not trust God because they did not know Him. They did not know Him because they were not seeking Him. They did not seek Him because they did not love Him. They wanted to work things out their own way and only wanted God around for what He could provide for them. They were unwilling to sacrifice for Him.

Unbelief is the biggest hindrance to our faith; it will hinder us from receiving God's best. It will cause us to disobey Him by not trusting His direction in our lives.

Take heed brethren, lest there be in any of you an evil heart of unbe-
lief, in departing from the living God. But exhort one another daily,
while it is called To day; lest any of you be hardened through the
deceitfulness of sin.

—Hebrews 3:12-13

We can find ourselves wandering in the desert never receiving the victory that is in Christ because we don't believe God's Word. Sin is so
deceitful that if we are not diligently seeking the Lord we can be easily
influenced by things other than the truth. If we are not continually
embracing the truth, we will easily start to believe other people's lies and
our own deceitful hearts. It will also cause us to live our lives responding to
fear instead of responding to faith. Just the fact that we have seen miracles
and have had numerous spiritual experiences does not mean that we know
the Lord. It does not mean that we are progressing in our faith with the
Lord. The children of Israel saw and experienced miracles on a daily basis,
and yet they did not know Him. Therefore, they did not believe His
promises and did not obey His command to enter into the Promised
Land.

It's not experiences that we should treasure but rather being with Jesus
on a daily basis and hearing from Him. We can have many experiences
with the Lord, but if we're not seeking and learning from Him daily, our
faith will not grow. We need to "grow in the grace and knowledge of our
Lord and Savior Jesus Christ" and not rest on our past experiences (2 Peter
3:18). If we are not seeking Him daily, then we are quick to forget what
the Lord did for us in the past. We also tend to look at our situation and
troubles in the natural and not through the eyes of faith.

In Matthew 17, Jesus took Peter, James, and John, His inner circle, up
onto a high mountain to pray. While Jesus was praying, He was transfigured before them and His face shone like the sun and His clothes were as
white as light. While Jesus was praying, Moses and Elijah appeared and
talked with Him. Then Peter said, "Lord, it is good for us to be here: if
thou wilt, let us make here three tabernacles; one for thee, and one for
Moses, and one for Elias [Elijah]" (v.4). But while Peter was speaking, a
bright cloud enveloped them and a voice interrupted him from the cloud

saying, "This is my beloved Son, in whom I am well pleased; hear ye him" (v.5). The Lord interrupted Peter while he was talking because it was not a time for his own thoughts and ideas. That's why God said "this is my beloved Son, hear ye him." In other words, take all direction from Jesus; He is the most important thing. As soon as the disciples heard this, they fell on their faces and were afraid. Then Jesus came up to them and touched them and said, "Arise, and be not afraid. And when they had lifted up their eyes, they saw no man, save Jesus only" (vv.7-8). They looked up and saw no man except for Jesus, which is the position God wants us to stay in. Otherwise our own thoughts and unfounded fears arise.

Commemorating past spiritual experiences can be a hindrance to our faith, like Peter wanting to build three tabernacles to commemorate the occasion. These things can end up like an Egypt in our lives, if we are continually looking back and not progressing forward in our faith. What happens is that those things end up being more than they really are. Or we end up trying to recreate the past, which always hinders the future. We need to treasure these mountaintop experiences, but not to look to or rely on them. We're daily to look to and rely on Christ only!

Peter wanted to make three tabernacles, thinking that Moses and Elijah were just as important as Jesus. But the voice stopped that thought and focused Peter on Jesus. It's not certain experiences that we should treasure but being with Jesus daily and hearing from Him. We can experience great miracles firsthand as Peter did and yet still have unbelief in our hearts.

As an example of this is, as soon as the thrill of seeing Jesus transfigured on the mountaintop was over, they were unable to cast a demon out of a man's son.

> And when they came to the crowd, a man came up to him and, kneeling before him, said, "Lord, have mercy on my son, for he is an epileptic and he suffers terribly. For often he falls into the fire, and often into the water. And I brought him to your disciples, and they could not heal him." And Jesus answered, "O faithless and twisted generation, how long am I to be with you? How long am I to bear with you? Bring him here to me." And Jesus rebuked him, and the

demon came out of him, and the boy was healed instantly. Then the disciples came to Jesus privately and said, "Why could we not cast it out?" He said to them, "Because of your little faith. For truly, I say to you, if you have faith like a grain of mustard seed, you will say to this mountain, 'Move from here to there,' and it will move, and nothing will be impossible for you." But this kind never comes out except by prayer and fasting.

—Matthew 17:14-21 (ESV)

The father brought his demon-possessed son to the disciples to be healed. The disciples could not heal the boy, so the man came to Jesus and asked Him to have mercy on his son and heal him. Jesus answered the man by rebuking His disciples and calling them a "faithless and twisted generation" referring to their unbelief, for their inability to heal the boy. Jesus gave the man his request and healed his son by casting a demon out of him. Then the disciples asked Jesus why they couldn't cast the demon out of the boy. Jesus replied, "Because of your little faith." He told them if they had faith the size of a mustard seed, they could say to a mountain move and it would move and nothing would be impossible for them. Then Jesus told them the key to having the faith and the authority we need as Christians: "But this kind never comes out except by prayer and fasting."

Jesus rebuked His disciples in front of the man to provoke them to have the kind of faith needed, the kind of faith He expected them to have. The disciples, ashamed of their powerlessness, wanted to know why they could not cast the demon out of the boy. Jesus told them they needed to fast and pray in order to have the faith and power needed.

This kind of faith only comes from a life of self-denial and prayer, which is what "fast" means—to deny or give up something and spend that time in prayer. To lead a life of "prayer and fasting" is to live a life of denying your own desires and ambitions and spending that time seeking the Lord. It is only by spending time with the Lord that our lives are transformed and our faith grows. The more time we spend with Jesus Christ in prayer and in the study of His Word, the more effective our prayers will be, because we will know Him and pray according to His will. The more time we spend building our relationship with the Lord, the more faith and power we will have because more of His life will be reflected through us. We can't expect our faith to grow if we are not spending significant time seeking the Lord. We can't expect our lives or other people's lives to change without spending time in prayer. Something is clearly wrong with our faith if we do not want to set things aside and spend time with Jesus Christ.

Most people lack the faith and the power needed to live a triumphant life, because they are so entranced by the things of this world that they have no time for prayer. They do not have a disciplined prayer life, because their love for other things takes precedence. This attitude manifests itself in unbelief and the lack of holiness in their lives. They have a hard time overcoming sin and temptation in their lives because they do not seek His deliverance. They are ignorant of God's Word and who Jesus is because they do not diligently study His Word. These people spend their whole lives stagnant never obtaining the promises available to them. "Faith cometh by hearing, and hearing by the word of God" (Rom. 10:17).

Our faith cannot grow without an intimate relationship with Jesus Christ. "The word was made flesh and dwelt amongst us" (John 1:14). The more we study the Word of God, the more we will know Jesus Christ and the more we will believe it. The more we believe in the Word of God, the more we will trust and act upon it. We need to study God's Word and take heed to what God spoke to Peter on the mountain when Jesus was transfigured. "This is my beloved Son, in whom I am well pleased; hear ye Him" (Matt. 17:5). Look for, follow, hear, learn from, and take all direction from Jesus.

The bottom line is that you can't speak for someone you don't know. You can't pray effectively according to God's will if you do not know His will (His Word). The authority we have as a believer is in knowing Jesus Christ. We have no power or authority apart from Him.

We see a good example of not knowing Jesus and therefore not having any authority in the story of "seven sons of Sceva" in Acts 19. In this story, some Jewish exorcists were trying to cast out demons in the name of the Lord Jesus by saying: "We adjure you by Jesus whom Paul preacheth" (v.13). The seven sons of Sceva, a priest, were among those who tried exorcising a demon out of a man in this way. The demon answered them: "Jesus I know, and Paul I know; but who are ye?" (v.15). Then the man who had the evil spirit attacked them so that they ran out of the house naked and wounded.

They could not cast the demon out of the man in Jesus' name because they had no authority to speak for Him. They had no authority because they did not know Jesus and were not intimate with Him. They tried to cast the demon out of the man by evoking Jesus' name, without knowing Jesus. If you truly know Jesus Christ, then you will have the authority to speak for Him. If you don't know Jesus, using His name will be mere words without meaning.

Just as in a marriage relationship, the more you get to know your partner, the more you can speak for them. You will learn what they like or dislike and what makes them happy or sad. You will also get to know their opinions on certain subjects as the relationship grows. Therefore, when someone else asks you what your partner might think on a certain subject, you can confidently answer correctly because you know your partner's opinion. You have been given the right to speak (authority) on their behalf because of your marriage relationship with them. You can act on your partner's behalf confidently and accurately without second-guessing yourself.

If we are not totally focused on Jesus Christ, our focus will be on the temporal things of this world and we will miss many opportunities for the Lord to work. If we are not seeking Him daily, we will easily forget what He has done for us in the past and will not have the faith that He will work in the future. When we are seeking the Lord daily by reading His Word and praying, our faith and trust in the Lord naturally increases because we know and understand who He is, what He wants, and what He expects. Then when the time of testing comes, we will keep focused on Jesus and trust Him no matter what things look like. The Lord wants our faith to continue to grow, for if our faith is growing, our relationship also is growing. "I press toward the mark for the prize of the high calling of God in Christ Jesus" (Phil. 3:14).

CHAPTER 6

▼

OBEDIENCE IS BETTER
THAN SACRIFICE

And Samuel said, Hath the LORD as great delight in burnt offerings and sacrifices, as in obeying the voice of the LORD? Behold, to obey is better than sacrifice, and to hearken than the fat of rams. For rebellion is as the sin of witchcraft, and stubbornness is as iniquity and idolatry. Because thou hast rejected the word of the LORD, he hath also rejected thee from being king.

—1 Samuel 15:22-23

Samuel was a prophet, priest, and judge to the people of Israel all of his life. When Samuel got old, he assigned his sons to be judges over Israel. But his sons were corrupt and did not follow God's Word as Samuel their father had. They were not faithful as their father had been in administering justice. They used their positions for monetary gain. "They took bribes and perverted justice" (1 Sam. 8:3 ESV).

The elders of Israel got together and said to Samuel: "Behold, you are old and your sons do not walk in your ways. Now appoint for us a king to judge us like all the nations" (v.5). Samuel did not like the elder's request and took it to prayer. The Lord told Samuel to give the people what they wanted "for they have not rejected you, but they have rejected me from being king over them" (v.7). From the beginning, the Lord wanted to be the sole ruler over the Israelites. Now they were rejecting Him once more just as they had rejected Him to serve other gods after He had brought them out of Egypt.

The Lord told Samuel to give them what they wanted, but to warn them of what it would be like to have a king to rule over them. So Samuel warned the people. The king would take their sons and use them to drive his chariots and be his horsemen. He would use them to farm his land and to make equipment for him. The king would take their daughters and use them as cooks and bakers. He would take the best of the land, the orchards and vineyards, and give them to his servants. He would take the best of the young men and the best of the young women for his work. "He will take the tenth of your flocks, and you shall be his slaves. And in that day you will cry out because of your king, whom you have chosen for yourselves, but the LORD will not answer you in that day" (1 Sam. 8:17-18).

After all this, the people still wanted a king to rule over them. They wanted a king so they could be like all the other nations who had kings. They also wanted a king to be their judge and to go out and fight their battles for them. The Lord told him to listen to them and give them a king. Then Samuel told all the elders to go back to their cities.

There was a wealthy man named Kish who was from the tribe of Benjamin. He had a son named Saul. In all of Israel there was not a man more handsome than Saul, nor was there any that stood taller than him.

Now Samuel called the people together to the LORD at Mizpah. And he said to the people of Israel, "Thus says the LORD, the God of Israel, 'I brought up Israel out of Egypt, and I delivered you from the hand of the Egyptians and from the hand of all the kingdoms that were oppressing you.' But today you have rejected your God, who saves you from all your calamities and your distresses, and you have said to him, 'Set a king over us.' Now therefore present yourselves before the LORD by your tribes and by your thousands."

—1 Samuel 10:17-19 (ESV)

All the tribes presented themselves before the Lord so a king could be selected out of them. Out of all the tribes of Israel, Benjamin was selected.

Through a process of selection within the tribe of Benjamin, Saul was selected. "And Samuel said to all the people, "Do you see him whom the LORD has chosen? There is none like him among all the people." And all the people shouted, "Long live the king!" (v.24). Then Samuel told them the rights and duties of the kingship and sent the people back to their homes.

The first major event Saul was responsible for was to rally all of Israel to fight against the Ammonites who had come to destroy the city of Jabesh-gilead. Saul and the people delivered Jabesh-gilead and destroyed the Ammonites. Then Samuel called all the people to go to Gilgal and renew the kingdom and establish Saul as king before the Lord. They sacrificed peace offerings before the Lord and Saul and all the people greatly rejoiced.

Samuel gave his final address to the people by telling them that he had given them a king as they requested. Then he asked the people to testify if he had ever defrauded them or done them any wrong. The people came back saying: "You have not defrauded us or oppressed us or taken anything from any man's hand" (12:4). Then Samuel exhorted them to obey the Lord.

And now behold the king whom you have chosen, for whom you have asked; behold, the LORD has set a king over you. If you will fear the LORD and serve him and obey his voice and not rebel against the commandment of the LORD, and if both you and the king who reigns over you will follow the LORD your God, it will be well. But if you will not obey the voice of the LORD, but rebel against the commandment of the LORD, then the hand of the LORD will be against you and your king. Now therefore stand still and see this great thing that the LORD will do before your eyes. Is it not wheat harvest today? I will call upon the LORD, that he may send thunder and rain. And you shall know and see that your wickedness is great, which you have done in the sight of the LORD, in asking for yourselves a king." So Samuel called upon the LORD, and the LORD sent thunder and rain that day, and all the people greatly feared the LORD and Samuel.

—1 Sam. 12:13-18 (ESV)

Samuel told the people of Israel that if they and their king obeyed the Lord, then their nation would be blessed. But if they and their king rebelled against the commands of the Lord "then the hand of the LORD will be against you and your king" (v.15). Samuel told them it was a very wicked thing for them to reject the Lord and want a king instead. He would show them how wicked that decision was by giving them a sign. The sign would be rain and thunder at the most inopportune time—during their wheat harvest. When you are harvesting wheat, the last thing you want is rain. So the Lord sent rain and thunder as a sign as Samuel had told them. The Lord wanted to show them through this sign that He was in control of everything. Their abundance of harvest and sustenance was controlled and given by the Lord. If they rejected Him as their Lord, He would take away their blessing. But if they served Him, He would bless them abundantly.

When the people saw the rain and thunder, they feared for their lives. They asked Samuel to pray for them, for this evil of asking for a king. Samuel told the people to not be afraid; the Lord was not going to destroy them even though they had done evil. He told them: "Do not turn aside from following the LORD, but serve the LORD with all your heart. And do not turn aside after empty things that cannot profit or deliver, for they are empty" (vv.20-21). The Lord would not forsake His chosen people for His name's sake. Samuel left the people that day with a warning. "Only fear the LORD and serve him faithfully with all your heart. For consider what great things he has done for you. But if you still do wickedly, you shall be swept away, both you and your king" (1 Sam. 12:24-25 ESV).

Everything was clearly laid out for the people that day. They were to follow the Lord with all of their heart. If they didn't serve the Lord, they would lose His blessing and be destroyed. The Lord blessed Saul as long as he was obedient, prospering him in everything that he did.

Saul chose 3,000 men to go up against the Philistines. Saul took 2,000 of the men to Michmash, while his son Jonathan took 1,000 to Gibeah. The Lord gave Saul's son Jonathan a military victory over the Philistines at Gibeah. When Saul heard about the victory, he blew the trumpet and called all the people of Israel to come out and join them at Gilgal. When the rest of the Philistines heard of the defeat, they assembled in Michmash "thirty thousand chariots and six thousand horsemen and troops like the sand of the seashore in multitude" (13:5).

When the men of Israel saw that the Philistines had come against them, they were scared and hid themselves "in caves and in holes and in rocks and in tombs and in cisterns, and some Hebrews crossed the fords of the Jordan to the land of Gad and Gilead" (vv.6-7). The people that followed Saul to Gilgal were trembling with fear.

Samuel told Saul to wait at Gilgal for seven days, and then they would make a sacrifice to the Lord and call upon Him for help. But Samuel did not show up after the seven allotted days, and Saul was getting restless because the people were scattering (v.8). The Lord used this waiting period to test Saul, because he was not wholeheartedly putting his trust in the Lord. Saul was also attributing the military victories he had to himself and not to the Lord. So he was tested to see if he would wait or take matters into his own hands.

So Saul took it upon himself to offer up sacrifices to the Lord, even though it was unlawful for anyone to do so other than the appointed priest. As soon as Saul finished making sacrifices to the Lord, Samuel showed up. If Saul had waited a little bit longer, everything would have been fine. But typical of a long and ongoing trial, he failed at the end because he grew weary of waiting.

> *Samuel said, "What have you done?" And Saul said, "When I saw that the people were scattering from me, and that you did not come within the days appointed, and that the Philistines had mustered at Michmash, I said, 'Now the Philistines will come down against me at Gilgal, and I have not sought the favor of the LORD.' So I forced myself, and offered the burnt offering." And Samuel said to Saul, "You have done foolishly. You have not kept the command of the LORD your God, with which he commanded you. For then the LORD would have established your kingdom over Israel forever. But now your kingdom shall not continue. The LORD has sought out a man after his own heart, and the LORD has commanded him to be prince*

over his people, because you have not kept what the LORD com-
manded you."

—1 Samuel 13:11-14 (ESV)

Instead of admitting to Samuel that what he did was wrong, Saul made excuses for why he did what he did. He blamed it on the fact that Samuel did not show up on time and he was pressed to do something because the people were leaving. He figured at this point he had to take matters into his own hands. Samuel told Saul that he disobeyed the Lord by taking it upon himself to make the sacrifice. Now the Lord, who was going to establish Saul as king over Israel forever, was going to take it away from him and give it to "a man after his own heart." Nevertheless, Saul remained as king until the new king who would take his place was raised up.

Samuel told Saul to listen to the words of the Lord: "Now go and strike Amalek and devote to destruction all that they have. Do not spare them, but kill both man and woman, child and infant, ox and sheep, camel and donkey" (1 Sam. 15:3). So Saul assembled the men together to fight against the Amalekites in accordance to the Word of the Lord. The Lord blessed them with a mighty victory over the Amalekites. Saul and his men killed everyone except for Agag the king and the best of the sheep and cattle.

Once again Saul disobeyed the Lord. He did not destroy everything as the Lord commanded. Instead he kept Agag and the best of the livestock alive. Saul felt so good about what he did in the battle that he set up a monument for himself in Carmel.

The Lord told Samuel that He regretted making Saul a king because "he has turned back from following me and has not performed my commandments" (v.11). When Samuel came to Saul to confront him on his disobedience, Saul immediately told Samuel: "I have performed the commandment of the LORD" (v.13). Samuel said to Saul "What then is this bleating of the sheep in my ears and the lowing of the oxen that I hear?" (v.14). Saul said, "the people spared" the best of the livestock to make sacrifices to the Lord.

Saul is typical of a hypocrite: He publicly boasts of his obedience and yet it is obvious (like the sound of the sheep and cattle in the background) that he is indulging in the flesh. He was also quick to pass the blame on to the people by saying "the people spared" the livestock. Saul also took it one step further by trying to justify his actions to Samuel by making it sound like he was doing it for God—by saying the livestock were saved to make "sacrifice to the LORD your God." Saul is typical of the self-righteous who try to justify themselves before all by showing how much they are serving the Lord. They do that by making what they are doing look and sound more spiritual. But to those who know the Word of God, their disobedience is manifestly clear.

> *And Samuel said, Hath the LORD as great delight in burnt offerings and sacrifices, as in obeying the voice of the LORD? Behold, to obey is better than sacrifice, and to hearken than the fat of rams. For rebellion is as the sin of witchcraft, and stubbornness is as iniquity and idolatry. Because thou hast rejected the word of the LORD, he hath also rejected thee from being king.*
>
> —1 Samuel 15:22-23

It is easier to make the outward sacrifice than to obey what the Lord is commanding. Obeying God's Word is better than the outward form of worship, service, or personal sacrifice. Saul sinned by putting his own conception of what was right above what God had told him. Sacrifice and service are worthless in His sight if it is not accompanied by obedience to His Word.

Samuel told Saul: "rebellion is as the sin of witchcraft." That is because rebellion is rejecting God and His divine direction over our lives. When we rebel, we attempt to determine the outcome of things other than God's way. We direct our lives according to our own will, not according to His will. We don't like God's Word, so we seek answers from other sources. Other sources are our own opinions, other people's wisdom, or even other religions. Rebellion is compared to "witchcraft"[1] because witchcraft, or divination, is seeking to manipulate people or future events by consulting the departing dead, like the use of fortune-tellers to look into the future.

Samuel rebuked Saul by confronting his sin and pointing out that obedience was better than sacrifice. Saul said to Samuel, "I have sinned, for I have transgressed the commandment of the LORD and your words, because I feared the people and obeyed their voice" (v.24 ESV). Instead of taking responsibility for his sin, Saul once again made excuses by blaming it on the people. Samuel said to him, "The LORD has torn the kingdom of Israel from you this day and has given it to a neighbor of yours, who is better than you." (v.28) Saul rejected the Lord, so the Lord rejected him. From this point on, the Lord's blessing and protection left Saul, so that Saul had to work hard to keep the kingdom together in his own strength.

Shortly after this, Samuel died and left Saul without council. The Philistines once again gathered to fight against Israel. When Saul saw how great their army was, he was restless, scared, and did not know what to do. So Saul inquired of the Lord, but the Lord did not answer him. "Then Saul said to his servants, 'Seek out for me a woman who is a medium, that I may go to her and inquire of her.' And his servants said to him, 'Behold, there is a medium at En-dor'" (1 Samuel 28:7).

Prior to Saul's downfall, he had "put the mediums and the necromancers out of the land" (v.3). But now he was telling his servants to find a medium so he could inquire of her. His servants told him of a medium in En-dor, so Saul disguised himself and went to the woman at night. Saul told the woman: "Divine for me by a spirit and bring up for me whomever I shall name to you" (v.8). She was reluctant to help because she didn't want to be caught and killed for divination. At first, she did not know it was Saul talking with her. But after he asked her to bring up Samuel, she knew it was Saul. She was afraid for her life, but Saul told her not to be afraid and asked her what she saw. "And she said, An old man cometh up; and he is covered with a mantle. And Saul perceived that it was Samuel, and he stooped with his face to the ground, and bowed himself" (v.14).

Then Samuel said to Saul, "Why have you disturbed me by bringing me up?" Saul answered, "I am in great distress, for the Philistines are warring against me, and God has turned away from me and answers me no more, either by prophets or by dreams. Therefore I have summoned you to tell me what I shall do." And Samuel said, "Why then do you ask me, since the LORD has turned from you and become your enemy? The LORD has done to you as he spoke by me, for the LORD has torn the kingdom out of your hand and given it to your neighbor, David. Because you did not obey the voice of the LORD and did not carry out his fierce wrath against Amalek, therefore the LORD has done this thing to you this day. Moreover, the LORD will give Israel also with you into the hand of the Philistines, and tomorrow you and your sons shall be with me. The LORD will give the army of Israel also into the hand of the Philistines."

—1 Samuel 28:15-19 (ESV)

The witch said she saw an old man "covered in a mantle." That was what the judges wore and obviously what Samuel wore. When Saul heard what the old man was wearing, he perceived that it was Samuel. Saul had come there to consult with this necromancer, which he knew was totally against God's Law (Deut. 18:9-14). He was no longer hearing from God and was so deceived that he thought he was actually talking to Samuel. He had come there disguised and in the cover of darkness, knowing that what he was doing was wrong. Now Satan was undercover deceiving Saul by disguising himself as Samuel. It is just like Satan to masquerade as someone and something else (2 Cor. 11:14). The old man masquerading as Samuel told Saul that the kingdom had been taken from him and given to David, because Saul disobeyed God's voice. He also told him that Israel would be defeated by the Philistines and "tomorrow you and your sons shall be with me" (v.19).

You would think that at this point Saul would repent and submit to God. You would also think he would call on the Lord all night long for his fate to change, but he didn't! The next day, he went out to battle obviously not believing what was said to him the night before, just as he had lived his whole life never believing God's Word.

The next day, Saul was wounded from an arrow in battle with the Philistines. He told his armor-bearer to kill him so he would not be captured and abused by the Philistines. The armor-bearer would not kill him, so Saul killed himself by falling on his sword.

The Lord rejected Samuel as king and chose David to take His place. The Lord chose David, because he was a "man after his own heart" (1 Sam. 13:14). From the moment that David was anointed king, He gained favor with God and man. Even though David was anointed king, he did not become king right away. David had to wait for all of God's promises to be fulfilled. During that process of waiting on God's promises, David had to go through numerous trials. Unlike Saul, who was given the kingdom right away with very little opposition, David had to wait and withstand a lot of testing and opposition. God wanted to teach David obedience. He wanted him to have explicit trust in His faithfulness and direction.

From the very beginning, David's attitude was opposite that of Saul's, for David remained faithful throughout. No matter what the situation was, he gave God the glory and accounted it as God's will for his life. Whether he was victorious in battle or fleeing from the enemy, he still worshiped and obeyed God no matter what. He trusted God that His promises would come to pass. Whether king or servant, rich or poor, healthy or sick, victorious or defeated, David would have served Him, because he was a man after God's own heart!

Saul did not have a heart after God; he wanted to do things his own way. He loved his high position and the power he gained from it, but he did not want to submit himself to the Lord. He loved the praises of man, more than the praises of God. He wanted all the glory for himself. Ultimately, he received no glory.

Characteristics of those with a heart after God:

1. They serve and obey God no matter what.

2. Their condition or position in life has no bearing on their relationship with Him.

3. Their daily quest is to know Him more.

4. Their most prized possession is their relationship with Jesus Christ.

5. They don't participate in anything that hinders or compromises their relationship with Jesus Christ.

The tendency when we lose momentum or spiritual power in our Christian walk is to resort to fleshly things to satisfy the spiritual vacancy in our lives and to get the answers we need. We quickly resort to worldly wisdom instead of going to the one who is quick to forgive and the one who will set us on the right path. Instead of recognizing the deficiency, repenting from it and running hard after the one who can restore our hearts, we go the way of the world alienating ourselves from God.

As we can see from Saul's life, as well as other examples in the Bible, there is a tendency to want to go back to Egypt (the world).

In the Bible, Egypt represents:

1. Worldly prosperity

2. Worldly solutions and answers

3. Worldly resources

4. Relying on the flesh, your own abilities

5. Directing your own life according to your own wisdom or the wisdom of others

In the Bible, a famine usually represents God's punishment or testing of His people. It is during the times of famine that our hearts will truly be manifest. If we find ourselves in a spiritual famine, it is what we do during those times that will determine our outcome. We have two options, we either go to Egypt (the world) for nourishment, or we go to Christ for real nourishment. When Saul found himself in a spiritual famine, he looked to the things of the world, not to self-examination and repentance. David, on the other hand, was always quick to repent and call upon God.

Worldly wisdom says that we must focus on our problems in order to find the solution. This is proved by the fact that we have an abundance of counselors, and yet nothing is ever fixed. Worldly philosophy says that we need to analyze and discuss our problems in order to overcome them. This wisdom causes us to think that our particular problem is causing our spiritual famine and lack of joy, when in reality our problems are not causing those things, but rather our lack of seeking hard after Jesus Christ.

Our bookstores are filled with self-help books. There are books dealing with every aspect of marital problem as well as every aspect of the problems associated with being single. There are books on how to overcome addictions as well as books telling us how to deal with those who are addicted. There are books dealing with all aspects of depression, loneliness, fear, anxiety, guilt, anger, unforgiveness, and betrayal. There are books on managing money and on how to stay out of debt, get out of debt, and have financial freedom. There are books to deal with virtually all problems we encounter in life. The book might add the spiritual side as part of the solution to the problem, yet the focus is still on the problem.

The real problem is that we can be like Saul. He was more worried about the battle than about being rightly related to God. He was focused on the problem ahead and, because of that, he was aggressively trying to pursue council relating to that. But, if he had focused on his relationship with the Lord, the rest would have easily fallen into divine order. If Saul's relationship with the Lord had been right, he would have easily defeated the enemy.

We must be careful not to emulate Saul's life by seeking council from other sources other than the Word of God. Saul got so bad that he was even willing to consult a witch to get answers. He didn't start out like that, but he ended up that way. The world's solutions are not centered around the Word of God but on human wisdom and ingenuity. They always focus on the problem, never focusing on the One who can fix the problem.

As Christians, we need to focus on the solution, our relationship with Jesus Christ. We need to study God's Word and apply that truth in our lives. If we seek any other solution other than the Word of God, our lives will be out of alignment with Jesus Christ. Then we will find ourselves in a famine, full of fear and unnecessary problems. We must make sure that our relationship with Jesus Christ is in right standing first before we pursue anything else. If we put our relationship first, then we are less likely to disobey God by pursuing our own interests.

It is painful to watch people who have purposely disobeyed the Lord then spend years, sometimes even a lifetime, focused on trying to correct the problem. The problem is that they never correct their problem, because they are never focused or submitted to the solution. Or they want God to fix the problems their disobedience caused, but they are unwilling to separate from or amend their lives in any way. Instead of forsaking their idolatry and lusts, they want God to bless them. Nothing good comes out of disobeying the Lord. We can be deceived thinking that everything is going fine in Egypt and miss the blessings of the Promised Land.

There is only one solution to guard against this error. That solution is to have a heart after God—to hunger and thirst for more of Him, not settling for anything less than God's fullness and complete blessing in your life.

> *As the hart panteth after the water brooks, so panteth my soul after thee, O God. My soul thirsteth for God, for the living God: when shall I come and appear before God?*
>
> —Psalm 42:1-2

> *Blessed are they which do hunger and thirst after righteousness: for they shall be filled.*
>
> —Matthew 5:6

David had a heart after God because he hungered and thirsted for more of Him. We can see his thirst for God in many of his psalms, such as in Psalm 42: "My soul thirsteth for God." God's Word tells us that those who hunger and thirst after righteousness shall be filled. Filled with what? They shall be filled with His Holy Spirit—His life. It is only through this intimate relationship that we have His divine life. Through the Holy Spirit's empowerment, we have the ability to live by the standards and principles that He has shown us in the Sermon on the Mount and throughout the Bible.

Our ability to separate from sin and worldliness is by having more of His life, His Spirit. His Spirit draws us, convicts us, leads and guides us, comforts us, and reveals Christ to us and in us. As we study the Word of God, the Holy Spirit reveals to us—speaks to us—and teaches us His

Word. It's this hunger for Jesus Christ that will keep us during life's ups and downs. The more we seek the Lord, the more He empowers us to obey Him by sanctifying our lives. The more our lives become sanctified, the less we will be tempted to disobey. The more we draw closer to the Lord, the clearer His Word will be and the more meaning it will have in our lives.

Today, when we read Scripture that refers to being "hungry or thirsty," we lose the original meaning. In this country, we have water and food available at our beck and call. When we are thirsty, we easily get something to drink, because we have drinking fountains, running water, soda machines, and convenience stores available everywhere. We also have an abundance of food in this nation, proved by our obesity rate. We also have the money to buy food. So when we are hungry, we don't give it a second thought; we buy something to eat. Getting food is convenient and easy. We go to the grocery store or snack machine, or we go to the drive-through. We are used to instant gratification. Most people in our nation have never had to go without food or water.

It is true that regardless of the abundance and convenience we have in this country, everyone still gets a little hungry or thirsty on a daily basis. But that is not the hunger and thirst that Jesus is talking about in Matthew 5:6: "Blessed are they which do hunger and thirst after righteousness: for they shall be filled." When Jesus taught this Scripture, He was living in a desert area that had very few water sources. People had to make trips to the well, river, or lake to get water. They had to fill up jars and buckets to transport the water back to their houses. There were no convenience stores, and water was a precious commodity. They didn't have indoor plumbing to bring the water into their homes, and they didn't have dishwashers and washing machines. If they took a trip, which they mostly did by foot, they had to carry enough water to get them through. Most towns were built around water sources such as springs, lakes, and rivers.

When I worked in Afghanistan, it made me wonder: Is this the way people lived in biblical times? In the remote villages of Afghanistan, it looks as though the people are still living the way they did 2,000 years ago—not progressing in modern amenities at all. They have a communal well in the middle of their small town where the people get their water. All the towns are located by rivers, so that goatherds, gardens, and livestock will have water. Not only do they water the livestock from these rivers, but they also wash their clothes and bath in them as well.

When the people get hungry, they must pick food out of the garden, slaughter an animal, or make their own bread. When preparing the food to be consumed, they do not have the conveniences we have. They have to spend a lot of time and work preparing the food. From start to finish, they grow, raise, and process all their food.

When Jesus was talking about "hunger and thirst," it meant more to the original listeners then it does today. When you talk to most of the villagers in Afghanistan, what they want most is more wells with potable water. Water is a precious commodity and necessary to stay alive and keep their gardens and livestock going. They do not take their water supply for granted—they protect it.

Being in the military, I have had times when I went without food and when water was scarce. One particular time stands out in my mind. This story helps explain the type of "thirst" Jesus was talking about. During a military exercise, we had a long movement on foot through the woods to our final objective. Each of us carried over a hundred pounds of equipment on our backs in our rucksacks. We had such a long trek that we planned on resupplying our water from the various streams on our way to the objective. Our map showed that there were numerous streams along our route. On this movement, each of us carried over eight quarts of water, but the water went fast considering the weight we were carrying in our rucksacks and the fact that it was hot—close to a 100 degrees outside.

Over the course of the excruciating maneuver, we drank all of our water, but according to our map we were only 750 meters from a stream. When we finally got to the stream, it was dried up. There was no water to be found, and we were thirsty. Water became our main focus as we studied the map for other nearby streams to resupply our water. The next stream we located on the map was 2,000 meters away. It was a larger, known water source; we would have to get there if we wanted to survive. So we headed for the stream. On the way to that water source, I was so thirsty that that's all I had on my mind. It was my total focus. While on the way, my head ached, my throat was dry, and I was starting to feel weak. All of us had the early signs of heat exhaustion, but we had to keep going toward the water if we were to survive.

At this point, we had nothing else on our minds but water, and nothing else would have satisfied us. No other worries or concerns entered our minds, nothing else mattered but getting water. We were oblivious to the things around us and did not care about our security or being seen and heard by the enemy because we were so thirsty. We had a "single eye" (focus) on getting water. At the time, it would not have mattered if the water source was a mud puddle, we would have drank from it. If we didn't get water soon, we would all be dead. When we finally made it to the stream and saw that it had water, we quickly drank in as much water as we could. As soon as the water started to flow in us, we could feel our lives coming back to us. The water refreshed us and gave us our energy back. We were so thankful for the water that we never took it for granted after this incident. We took great care in planning water stops and resupplies in our future operations.

That is the kind of hunger and thirst that Jesus talked about. Our total focus needs to be on Him, our source. We need this source in order to stay alive and survive. We want this source more than anything else and nothing else will satisfy. To "hunger and thirst" for Jesus Christ is to be totally focused on Him—to have a single eye. Jesus said, "Blessed are those which do hunger and thirst after righteousness: for they shall be filled" (Matt. 5:6).

When we are seeking Jesus Christ and are focused on Him, He fills us with His life and His life produces fruit. His life renews and sanctifies us as we seek Him. To not seek Jesus Christ is to cut ourselves off from the source—this source is life! "He that hath the Son hath life: and he that hath not the Son of God hath not life" (1 John 5:12)

The light of the body is the eye: therefore when thine eye is single, thy whole body also is full of light: but when thine eye is evil, thy body also is full of darkness.

—Luke 11:34 (ESV)

CHAPTER 7

▼

DO NOT BE UNEQUALLY
YOKED WITH
UNBELIEVERS!

Do not be unequally yoked with unbelievers. For what partnership has righteousness with lawlessness? Or what fellowship has light with darkness? What accord has Christ with Belial? Or what portion does a believer share with an unbeliever? What agreement has the temple of God with idols? For we are the temple of the living God; as God said, "I will make my dwelling among them and walk among them, and I will be their God, and they shall be my people. Therefore go out from their midst, and be separate from them, says the Lord, and touch no unclean thing; then I will welcome you, and I will be a father to you, and you shall be sons and daughters to me, says the Lord Almighty."

—2 Corinthians 6:14-18 (ESV)

The Lord told Abraham to leave his people and country and go to the land of Canaan. "I will make of you a great nation, and I will bless you and make your name great, so that you will be a blessing. I will bless those who bless you, and him who dishonors you I will curse, and in you all the families of the earth shall be blessed" (Gen. 12:2-3). Abraham obeyed the Lord and took with him his wife Sarai and his brother's son Lot and set out for the land of Canaan. When Abraham came into the land of Canaan he arrived at a place called Shechem where the Lord appeared to him. The Lord said "'To your offspring I will give this land.' So he built there an altar to the LORD, who had appeared to him" (Gen. 12:7). From there Abraham moved to the hill country east of Bethel and pitched his tent. His tent was pitched with Bethel to the west and Ai to the east. While he was there, he built an altar and "called upon the name of the Lord" (v.8).

God tested Abraham to see what he would do by sending a famine to the land of Canaan. Remember, a famine usually represented a time of testing and discipline for God's people, to see if they would wait to hear from God and get direction from Him or get restless and go the way of the world (Egypt). Egypt represents worldly prosperity, enablement, and security. God told Abraham to go to the land of Canaan where He would prosper him. Instead of waiting for God's provision to sustain him through the famine or waiting on God to direct him to some other location, Abraham decided to go to Egypt. Abraham chose the way of the flesh (Egypt), instead of going the way of the spirit (waiting on God's direction). He went to Egypt where the land was always fertile with plenty of food and water.

As they were about to enter into Egypt, Abraham feared that the Egyptians would kill him for his wife because she was so beautiful. So he told Sarai to lie to the Egyptians by telling them that she was his sister, not his wife. That way they would not kill him for her. Instead of killing him, they would treat him well because he was her brother.

When they entered Egypt, the Egyptians did see that Sarai was very beautiful. When the princes of the Pharaoh saw her, they told the Pharaoh how beautiful she was. She was taken into the Pharaoh's house. The Pharaoh treated Abraham very well because of Sarai and gave him sheep, oxen, donkeys, camels, and servants.

But the LORD afflicted Pharaoh and his house with great plagues because of Sarai, Abram's wife. So Pharaoh called Abram and said, "What is this you have done to me? Why did you not tell me that she was your wife? Why did you say, 'She is my sister,' so that I took her

for my wife? Now then, here is your wife; take her, and go." And
Pharaoh gave men orders concerning him, and they sent him away
with his wife and all that he had.

—Genesis 12:17-20 (ESV)

God afflicted Pharaoh's house with plagues because of Abraham's wife.
God intervened before Pharaoh took Sarai to be his wife and slept with
her. Both Abraham's and Sarai's compromises and lies were about to cost
them everything! But God stepped in and delivered them. Obviously,
Sarai's beauty was a stumbling block. She shouldn't have allowed the relationship with Pharaoh to escalate this far. Abraham was rebuked by a heathen king and by his lying made the one true God look bad. Abraham was
a poor witness to the heathen people around him. Then Pharaoh sent
them out of the land with all the stuff they had accumulated. If God had
not stopped this catastrophe and forced them to leave, they might have
stayed in Egypt and forgotten about the promise and the Promised Land.

So Abraham left Egypt with his wife and his brother's son Lot. They
journeyed back to the exact spot where they had started before they left for
Egypt—between Bethel and Ai. Once he arrived there, Abraham "called
on the name of the Lord" where he had first made an altar. Abraham was
back to the place where God had wanted him, in the land of Canaan, calling upon the Lord.

Lot also had large flocks and herds of livestock, so much so that the land
could not support both of them together. Because of that, there was a lot
of fighting between the herdsmen of Abraham and the herdsmen of Lot.
Then Abraham decided that they should separate so that the fighting for
space between them would stop.

And Lot lifted up his eyes and saw that the Jordan Valley was well
watered everywhere like the garden of the LORD, like the land of
Egypt, in the direction of Zoar. (This was before the LORD destroyed
Sodom and Gomorrah.) So Lot chose for himself all the Jordan Val-
ley, and Lot journeyed east. Thus they separated from each other.
Abram settled in the land of Canaan, while Lot settled among the

cities of the valley and moved his tent as far as Sodom. Now the men of Sodom were wicked, great sinners against the LORD.

—Genesis 13:10-13 (ESV)

Abraham gave Lot the decision to go in any direction and choose the land he wanted. If he went left, Abraham would go right; if he went right, Abraham would go left. Lot looked at the Jordan Valley and saw that it was well watered and reminded him of Egypt. The Jordan Valley had many cities of commerce. So Lot chose to live among the cities in the Jordan Valley and settled in Sodom. Abraham settled in the land of Canaan away from the cities and the inhabitants of the land.

Lot chose to live in the Jordan Valley because it reminded him of Egypt. Not only did it have plush land with plenty of water, but it also had thriving cities with businesses and people. He lusted for the lifestyle he had in Egypt, so he settled in the city of Sodom. Sodom offered many modern conveniences, people, entertainment, business opportunities, and the security that a big city brought. Abraham, on the other hand, lived in Canaan away from the cities with all of their evil influences. He lived in the quiet and secluded plains of Canaan. Lot obviously did not want the boring life of living out on the plains. He lusted after the hustle and bustle of the city life. The Scriptures tell us that the "the men of Sodom were wicked, great sinners against the LORD" (v.13).

Almost immediately after Lot moved to the city of Sodom, he was caught away with the problems that city had. Four kings had come up to fight against the king of Sodom and the king of Gomorrah who had with them three other kings. Sodom and Gomorrah were defeated and all the possessions of its cities were taken away. "They also took Lot, the son of Abram's brother, who was dwelling in Sodom, and his possessions, and went their way" (14:12). A person who had escaped capture came and told Abraham the news.

When Abraham heard that Lot and his entire household had been taken captive, he led 318 of his trained men to go after them. When he caught up with the enemy, he divided his force and attacked them by night defeating them. Abraham freed all the people and their possessions, including Lot and his family. Lot returned to the city of Sodom and continued to stay there despite the problems it brought on himself and his family.

Now Sarai, Abram's wife, had borne him no children. She had a female Egyptian servant whose name was Hagar. And Sarai said to Abram, "Behold now, the LORD has prevented me from bearing children. Go in to my servant; it may be that I shall obtain children by her." And Abram listened to the voice of Sarai. So, after Abram had lived ten years in the land of Canaan, Sarai, Abram's wife, took Hagar the Egyptian, her servant, and gave her to Abram her husband as a wife. And he went in to Hagar, and she conceived. And when she saw that she had conceived, she looked with contempt on her mistress. And Sarai said to Abram, "May the wrong done to me be on you! I gave my servant to your embrace, and when she saw that she had conceived, she looked on me with contempt. May the LORD judge between you and me!" But Abram said to Sarai, "Behold, your servant is in your power; do to her as you please." Then Sarai dealt harshly with her, and she fled from her.

—Genesis 16:1-6 (ESV)

Abraham didn't have a son yet to carry out the promises that God had given him. "To your offspring I will give this land" (Gen. 12:7). Sarai had not given Abraham a son and was anxious to have children to take away her reproach and fulfill this promise. They had been living in the land of Canaan for ten years and grew tired of waiting for this promised offspring. Sarai had an Egyptian slave named Hagar, who she probably received while she was in Egypt. Instead of waiting for God to fulfill the promise of giving her a son, Sarai decided to take matters into her own hands and offered her slave to her husband to be his wife. That way Sarai could have children through Hagar. The custom during this time period was to have multiple wives and for the wives to give up their slaves to their husbands, so they could have surrogate children through them. This custom was against God's Word and was not His promised plan for their lives.

Sarai told Abraham to sleep with Hagar so that she could have surrogate children through her. Instead of trusting and waiting for God's promises to come to fruition, Abraham listened to his wife. He got tired of waiting. Maybe the thought of having children through Hagar seemed logical to him, since it seemed impossible that a son would come any other way. So Abraham slept with Hagar, and she became pregnant.

Hagar was Sarai's slave, but as soon as she became pregnant she looked on Sarai with contempt and despised her. Hagar was obviously full of herself because she had accomplished what Sarai was unable to do, give Abraham an heir—so she looked down on Sarai because of her barrenness. Instead of Sarai admitting that she had made a mistake by talking Abraham into sleeping with Hagar, she blamed Abraham for Hagar's behavior. "May the wrong done to me be on you! I gave my servant to your embrace, and when she saw that she had conceived, she looked on me with contempt. May the LORD judge between you and me!" (v.5). Abraham possibly was treating Hagar with a little more honor now that she had conceived his baby, making Sarai jealous. Nevertheless, Abraham told Sarai that Hagar was her servant, so she could do to Hagar whatever she thought was right. So Sarai "dealt harshly with her, and she fled from her" (v.6).

Hagar fled into the wilderness to get away from Sarai who was treating her harshly. The angel of the Lord found her by a spring and asked her what she was doing. She said, "I am fleeing from my mistress Sarai" (v.8). The angel of the Lord told Hagar to return and submit to Sarai. Then the angel of the Lord gave her a promise "I will surely multiply your offspring so that they cannot be numbered for multitude" (v.10). He told her that she would have a son and should call him Ishmael. The angel of the Lord told Hagar what kind of man Ishmael would be: "He shall be a wild donkey of a man, his hand against everyone and everyone's hand against him, and he shall dwell over against all his kinsmen" (v.12). Ishmael descendants would also live next to his brother Isaac's descendants. This surely describes the Arab race that came from the descendents of Ishmael, children of the flesh (Ishmael), who would live next to the children of the promise (Isaac). Hagar went back and submitted to Sarai and bore Abraham a son and called his name Ishmael.

When Abram was ninety-nine years old the LORD appeared to Abram and said to him, "I am God Almighty; walk before me, and be blameless, that I may make my covenant between me and you, and may multiply you greatly." Then Abram fell on his face. And God said to him, "Behold, my covenant is with you, and you shall be the father of a multitude of nations. No longer shall your name be called Abram, but your name shall be Abraham, for I have made you the father of a multitude of nations. I will make you exceedingly fruitful, and I will make you into nations, and kings shall come from you. And I will establish my covenant between me and you and your offspring after you throughout their generations for an everlasting covenant, to be God to you and to your offspring after you. And I will give to you and to your offspring after you the land of your sojournings, all the land of Canaan, for an everlasting possession, and I will be their God."

—Genesis 17:1-8 (ESV)

God appeared to Abraham and reconfirmed the promise He had made to him. Abraham would be a father of many nations and kings would come from him. God would give Abraham and his offspring the land of Canaan "for an everlasting possession." God also changed Abram's name to Abraham and Sarai's name to Sarah.

God told Abraham that He would give him a son by Sarah his wife. Through Sarah many nations and kings would come. Abraham laughed "and said to himself, 'Shall a child be born to a man who is a hundred years old? Shall Sarah, who is ninety years old, bear a child?'" (v.17). Then Abraham offered up his son Ishmael to God to be his heir instead. "God said, 'No, but Sarah your wife shall bear you a son, and you shall call his name Isaac. I will establish my covenant with him as an everlasting covenant for his offspring after him.... I will establish my covenant with Isaac, whom Sarah shall bear to you at this time next year'" (vv.19-21).

The Lord appeared to Abraham as he was sitting outside his tent during the heat of the day. Abraham looked up and saw three men standing not too far from his tent. When Abraham saw them, he ran and bowed down to them and said "O Lord, if I have found favor in your sight, do not pass by your servant" (18:3). Abraham wanted them to stop and rest, while he prepared some food for them. They granted Abraham his request and stayed with him. While they were waiting for the food to be ready, they asked Abraham where Sarah his wife was. Abraham told them that Sarah was in the tent. "The LORD said, 'I will surely return to you about this time next year, and Sarah your wife shall have a son.' And Sarah was listening at the tent door behind him" (v.10). When Sarah heard this, she laughed because she was advanced in years and past the age of being able to bear children. The Lord asked Abraham why Sarah had laughed. He told Abraham: "Is anything too hard for the LORD? … I will return to you about this time next year, and Sarah shall have a son" (v.14). After the men were finished eating, they set out toward Sodom, and Abraham walked them out of the camp.

> The LORD said, "Shall I hide from Abraham what I am about to do, seeing that Abraham shall surely become a great and mighty nation, and all the nations of the earth shall be blessed in him? For I have chosen him, that he may command his children and his household after him to keep the way of the LORD by doing righteousness and justice, so that the LORD may bring to Abraham what he has promised him." Then the LORD said, "Because the outcry against Sodom and Gomorrah is great and their sin is very grave, I will go down to see whether they have done altogether according to the outcry that has come to me. And if not, I will know." So the men turned from there and went toward Sodom, but Abraham still stood before the LORD.
>
> —Genesis 18:17-22 (ESV)

The Lord told Abraham that He was going to go down and see if Sodom and Gomorrah's sin was as bad as He had heard. If their sin was as bad as reported, He was going to utterly destroy those cities along with their inhabitants. When Abraham heard this, he began to petition the Lord to spare the righteous in the city.

Abraham asked the Lord if He was going to destroy the righteous with the wicked. He asked the Lord if he would utterly destroy the cities if there were 50 righteous. The Lord told Abraham: "If I find at Sodom fifty righteous in the city, I will spare the whole place for their sake" (v.26). Abraham pressed the Lord even further: Would He destroy the city if there were 45 righteous? The Lord told Abraham He would spare the cities if there were 45 righteous. Abraham spoke again to the Lord: What if there were only 40 righteous? The Lord said that for the sake of the 40, He would not destroy Sodom and Gomorrah. Abraham asked the Lord again what He would do if there were 30 righteous. The Lord said He would not destroy them for 30. Abraham asked the Lord about 20 and then about 10 righteous. The Lord said He would not destroy the cities if there were 10 righteous there. The Lord finished speaking with Abraham and went away.

The two angels came to Sodom in the evening. When Lot saw them, He bowed down to them and invited them to stay at his house. At first they told him they wanted to spend the night in the town square, but Lot changed their minds and convinced them to spend the night at his house. So they stayed that night in Lot's house.

> But before they lay down, the men of the city, the men of Sodom, both young and old, all the people to the last man, surrounded the house. And they called to Lot, "Where are the men who came to you tonight? Bring them out to us, that we may know them." Lot went out to the men at the entrance, shut the door after him, and said, "I beg you, my brothers, do not act so wickedly. Behold, I have two daughters who have not known any man. Let me bring them out to you, and do to them as you please. Only do nothing to these men, for they have come under the shelter of my roof." But they said, "Stand back!" And they said, "This fellow came to sojourn, and he has become the judge! Now we will deal worse with you than with them." Then they pressed hard against the man Lot, and drew near to break the door down. But the men reached out their hands and brought Lot into the house with them and shut the door. And they struck with blindness the men who were at the entrance of the house, both small and great, so that they wore themselves out groping for the door.
>
> —Genesis 19:4-11 (ESV)

Sodom was filled with wickedness. The men of the city, both young and old, surrounded Lot's house and demanded that Lot send out the two visitors so that they could rape (sodomize) them. It is from the city of

Sodom and the perverted men who lived there that we get the word *sodomize*. The men were so wicked and perverse that they had given themselves over to homosexuality, thus bringing judgment upon them. When society is given over to homosexual perversion and accepts it as normal behavior, it is on the brink of judgment. That is why the angels were there to deliver Lot's family and get them out of there before they destroyed every last one of those wicked people.

Lot pleaded with the men of the city not to do this wickedness because these men were his guests. Obviously living in that wicked city had a vexing effect on Lot and had warped his thinking. Lot offered his daughters to the wicked men instead of his visitors so they could rape them. Lot sacrificed his family to live among these wicked people and now we see Lot was even willing to give his virgin daughters over to be raped to appease them. They asked Lot who he was to judge them. "Now we will deal worse with you than with them" (v.9). Then the wicked men tried to push aside Lot and break down the door of his house to get in. But the two angels pulled Lot back into the house and struck the men with blindness so that they could not find the door.

The angels asked Lot if he had any more family members in the city. "For we are about to destroy this place, because the outcry against its people has become great before the LORD, and the LORD has sent us to destroy it" (v.13). So Lot went and warned his sons-in-law who were to marry his daughters to get out of the city because God was going to destroy it. But they thought he was joking and did not take his warning seriously. When the morning arrived, the angels urged Lot to take his wife and daughters and get out, otherwise they would be swept away with the city when judgment came. Even so, after Lot had been warned by the angels to get out immediately, Lot still "lingered" (v.16). What was it about the place that they loved so much they were apprehensive to leave? Maybe Lot lingered because he had a hard time convincing his wife and daughters they needed to leave. Nevertheless, the angels took the hands of Lot, his wife, and two daughters and brought them out of the city. "And as they brought them out, one said, 'Escape for your life. Do not look back or stop anywhere in the valley. Escape to the hills, lest you be swept away'" (v.17). After the angels brought them out of the city, they told them to escape to the hills and not look back or stop anywhere in the valley.

> *Then the LORD rained on Sodom and Gomorrah sulfur and fire from the LORD out of heaven. And he overthrew those cities, and all the valley, and all the inhabitants of the cities, and what grew on the ground. But Lot's wife, behind him, looked back, and she became a pillar of salt. And Abraham went early in the morning to the place where he had stood before the LORD. And he looked down toward Sodom and Gomorrah and toward all the land of the valley, and he looked and, behold, the smoke of the land went up like the smoke of a furnace. So it was that, when God destroyed the cities of the valley, God remembered Abraham and sent Lot out of the midst of the over-throw when he overthrew the cities in which Lot had lived.*
>
> —Genesis 19:24-29 (ESV)

Even after the angels had warned them not to look back, Lot's wife dis-obeyed and was turned into a pillar of salt. The destruction of the cities in the valley was so devastating that all that remains there until today is the Dead Sea. It was so devastating that it is mentioned several times in the Bible as an example of judgment.

Lot escaped to the hills and lived in a cave with his two daughters. The older daughter said to the younger daughter, our father is old and there is no man to give us a child to preserve our family line. Let's get our father drunk, so we can sleep with him and get pregnant and have children by him. So they got their Father drunk and the oldest daughter slept with him. Lot was so drunk that he did not know that his oldest daughter had sex with him. The next night they got their father drunk again, and the youngest daughter slept with her father. "Thus both the daughters of Lot became pregnant by their father. The firstborn bore a son and called his name Moab. He is the father of the Moabites to this day. The younger also bore a son and called his name Ben-ammi. He is the father of the Ammo-nites to this day" (Gen. 19:36-38 ESV)

You would think it could not have gotten any worse for Lot's family, but it did. Their mother disobeyed the Lord by looking back and was turned into a pillar of salt. Then their father got so drunk two nights in a row that he did not realize that he was having incestuous sex with his daughters. His two daughters thought it logical to trick their father into getting drunk so they could become pregnant by him. The Scriptures become very silent concerning Lot's life after this incident, no more is said about him. Lot's daughters gave birth to two nations that would live next to Israel—the Moabites and the Ammonites.

The next year, at the appointed time when the Lord had said Sarah would have a child, she gave birth to a son named Isaac. Isaac was the off-spring God had promised Abraham, who Abraham waited for all these years.

When Isaac was weaned, Abraham made a big feast to celebrate the occasion. But during the celebration, Sarah saw Ishmael the son of Hagar the Egyptian laughing at Isaac. "So she said to Abraham, 'Cast out this slave woman with her son, for the son of this slave woman shall not be heir with my son Isaac'" (21:10). Abraham did not like what Sarah said because he loved his son Ishmael. "But God said to Abraham, 'Be not displeased because of the boy and because of your slave woman. Whatever Sarah says to you, do as she tells you, for through Isaac shall your offspring be named. And I will make a nation of the son of the slave woman also, because he is your offspring" (vv.12-13). So Abraham got up early in the morning and gave Hagar some food and water and sent her and Ishmael away. They departed and wandered in the wilderness of Beersheba. It was obviously hard for Abraham to send away his son, but he obeyed the Lord. He had experienced many years of walking with the Lord and had seen the fruit of disobedience as well as the fruit of obedience. Abraham had arrived at the point in his life that he knew God's way was perfect no matter what—no matter how it looked or felt.

After these things, God tested Abraham by telling him to offer up his son Isaac as a burnt offering on Mount Moriah. So Abraham took his son Isaac and some wood for the burnt offering to the place appointed by the Lord. On the third day, they arrived at a location where they could see the place where he was to be sacrificed. Abraham told his servants to stay there while he and his son Isaac went up to the sacrifice site. He told them they would return when they were finished offering up the sacrifice. On their way up, Isaac asked his father where the lamb for the burnt offering was. Abraham told Isaac: "God will provide for himself the lamb for a burnt offering" (Gen. 22:8).

> *When they came to the place of which God had told him, Abraham built the altar there and laid the wood in order and bound Isaac his son and laid him on the altar, on top of the wood. Then Abraham reached out his hand and took the knife to slaughter his son.*
> *But the angel of the LORD called to him from heaven and said, "Abraham, Abraham!" And he said, "Here am I." He said, "Do not lay your hand on the boy or do anything to him, for now I know that you fear God, seeing you have not withheld your son, your only son, from me." And Abraham lifted up his eyes and looked, and behold, behind him was a ram, caught in a thicket by his horns. And Abraham went and took the ram and offered it up as a burnt offering instead of his son.*
>
> —Genesis 22:9-13 (ESV)

God tested Abraham by telling him to sacrifice his son, his most prized possession. Abraham did not withhold anything from God, but obeyed Him and proved that he loved the Lord more than he loved his son. Abraham also believed the promise that through Isaac, God was going to make a mighty nation. He even believed that if Isaac was sacrificed, God was able to raise him up again. "By faith Abraham, when he was tested, offered up Isaac, and he who had received the promises was in the act of offering up his only son, of whom it was said, 'Through Isaac shall your offspring be named.' He considered that God was able even to raise him from the dead, from which, figuratively speaking, he did receive him back" (Heb. 11:17-19). The angel of the Lord stopped Abraham from sacrificing his son and God provided a ram to be sacrificed in his place. On this very spot on Mount Moriah, King Solomon would later build a temple where sacrifices would be made. This would also be the place where the ultimate sacrifice would be made. Jesus Christ took our place and was sacrificed for us, just as the ram was sacrificed for Isaac on Mount Moriah, Calvary.

Do not be unequally yoked with unbelievers. For what partnership has righteousness with lawlessness? Or what fellowship has light with darkness? What accord has Christ with Belial? Or what portion does a believer share with an unbeliever? What agreement has the temple of God with Idols? For we are the temple of the living God; as God said, "I will make my dwelling among them and walk among them, and I will be their God, and they shall be my people. Therefore go out among their midst, and be separate from them, says the Lord, and touch no unclean thing; then I will welcome you, and I will be a father to you, and you shall be sons and daughters to me, says the Lord Almighty."

—2 Corinthians 6:14-18 (ESV)

We see, from looking at Abraham and Lot's lives, the evil that comes from living near and adapting to nonbelievers. From the very start, going to Egypt hurt them. From Abraham lying to Pharaoh and bringing back Hagar the Egyptian—to not trusting and obeying God. Abraham relied on the people and the amenities in Egypt to get him through the famine, not on God. Abraham left Egypt only because the Pharaoh told him to leave for all of the trouble he had caused. Living in Egypt ruined Lot and his wife and there was nothing but backsliding from that point on. There was something about Egypt that they loved, for their heart stayed in Egypt. They chose to live in Sodom because it reminded them of Egypt. They "lingered" when the angels told them to leave, because they didn't want to leave Sodom or see it destroyed. Lot's wife disobeyed the Lord and looked back at Sodom when they were fleeing and was turned into a pillar of Salt. Lot and his daughters were so warped by being "unequally yoked with unbelievers" that they thought it logical to have incestuous sex to carry on the family line.

As Christians, we are not to be unequally yoked with unbelievers. To be unequally yoked has reference to Leviticus 19:19 where it refers to not mixing unlike things together, because they will work against each other. For example, you don't want to team up an ox with a donkey to plow a field, because they will work against each other since they are two totally different animals used for two different functions. Also, you do not want your cattle to breed with any other animals, or otherwise its offspring would be an abomination and grotesque. You don't want to plant a field with mixed seed; it will be difficult to take care of, and come harvest time it will be impossible to separate.

The command to be a separate people was a very specific command given to the Israelites. From the beginning, God wanted the Israelites to remain separate from the heathen nations around them. When they entered into the Promised Land, God told the children of Israel to utterly destroy the inhabitants. The inhabitants of the land were a pagan people and God did not want their evil influence on His chosen people. So He told them to kill every one of them. God did not want them to make a covenant or treaty with them or to show mercy toward them in any way. He commanded them not to marry these pagan people and not to give their sons and daughters to them to marry (Deut. 7:2-3).

God was very specific to the Israelites concerning separation, just as He is with us today. He did not want the heathen nations to have an influence on them in any way. God knew that if the children of Israel mixed in with the people, they would be influenced by them, and eventually they would be turned away to serve other gods. The same holds true today. God wants us to remain separate from the evil influences and philosophies of the world and to be united with Christ. So to not be unequally yoked is not to be united with any unbeliever for a common purpose.

Jesus associated with sinners for one purpose only: to convict them of sin so that they would repent and be restored to God. Not to socialize and form alliances with them or to appease them in any way for friendship's sake. We associate with nonbelievers every day, but they should not be our closest friends; we should not date them, marry them, or partner in business with them. Our association with them should be for one purpose and that is to lead them to Christ. If we are hanging around nonbelievers and are not proactive in leading them to Christ, or we are not witnessing to them because we want to fit in and be liked, then ultimately we will be influenced by them and our faith will be neutered. We will pick up their likes and dislikes, their beliefs and philosophies. Eventually, in the end, what was once godly in our lives will be given over to sin.

As Christians, we need to make a conscious effort to separate from the evil influences that hinder our faith. We need to separate from the things in our society that work contrary to growth in our relationship with Jesus Christ. If we don't, those things will grab our hearts and minds and will ruin our faith. Not only will it breed complacency, but it will cause us to accept and make excuses for certain sins. If we don't separate from sin and compromise in our lives, we will ruin the next generation, our children. If we do not make a stand, each successive generation will become worse.

We need to guard our hearts and minds from:

1. What we watch

2. What we listen to

3. What we read

4. What we participate in

5. What we spend our money on

6. How we manage our time

7. Who we hang around with

8. Who we date

9. Who we marry

10. Who we take advice from—People of the world usually tell us what we want to hear. They appease the flesh. Their standards and answers are not based on the truth of God's Word.

Therefore, preparing your minds for action, and being sober-minded, set your hope fully on the grace that will be brought to you at the revelation of Jesus Christ. As obedient children, do not be conformed to the passions of your former ignorance, but as he who called you is holy, you also be holy in all your conduct, since it is written, "You shall be holy, for I am holy."

—1 Peter 1:13-14 (ESV)

"All flesh is like grass and all its glory like the flower of grass. The grass withers, and the flower falls, but the word of the Lord remains forever."

—1 Peter 1:24-25 (ESV)

▼

DON'T BE A HEARER WHO
FORGETS, BUT A DOER
WHO ACTS!

Then his mother and his brothers came to him, but they could not reach him because of the crowd. And he was told, "Your mother and your brothers are standing outside, desiring to see you." But he answered them, "My mother and my brothers are those who hear the word of God and do it."

—Luke 8:19-21 (ESV)

For whosoever shall do the will of my Father which is in heaven, the same is my brother, and sister, and mother.

—Matthew 12:50 (KJV)

Our lives are made up of a series of days. There are seven days in a week, 30 days in a month, and 365 days in a year. Seven days make up one week, four weeks make up one month, and twelve months make up one year, and many years make up our lives. Every day that God has given us is precious, vital, and significant.

How we make use of our day or how we spend our time during that day will effect how our day will be tomorrow. The decisions we make today, whether they are good or bad, will effect how our day will be tomorrow, next week, and next year. As a matter of fact, how we start out our mornings usually affects how the rest of our day will be. If it starts out bad, we usually have to put forth a lot of effort in order to change that negative direction.

Those decisions we make, or those daily habits, whether good or bad, if repeated will not only affect tomorrow but will affect next week, next month, and next year. If we make a bad decision or continue in sin, it could affect the rest or our lives, bring us into deeper bondage, and cause us to make even worse decisions because we have strayed so far from the right way to live. These bad decisions and sinful habits will not only affect the rest of our lives, but our eternal state as well.

If we don't change today, we can't expect to be changed tomorrow—we will be the same! If we do nothing today, how will something other than nothing happen tomorrow?

For when tomorrow arrives, we will be living another new day and will be at the same decision point. No matter what we do or don't do, time will go by. If we have a goal that takes two years to complete and we don't start today, we won't complete it in two years, but the two years will pass by anyway. At the end of those two years, we will be wishing that we had started that goal because we would have completed it. But we didn't—we put it off another day.

We need to honestly sit down and analyze our daily walk with Jesus Christ and make sure we are not withholding anything back from serving Him. "Examine yourselves, to see whether you are in the faith. Test yourselves. Or do you not realize this about yourselves, that Jesus Christ is in you?—unless indeed you fail to meet the test!" (2 Cor. 13:5 ESV) Didn't Jesus tell us that those who "hear the word of God and do it" are the same as His brother, sister, and mother (Luke 8:21; Matt 12:50)?

Consider your normal day and analyze your faith with these questions.

1. When you wake up in the morning, do you spend time in prayer thanking God for a brand-new day, praying for His help and divine direction for the day?

2. How much time do you spend each day alone with the Lord, praying and studying His Word?

3. Are you knowingly disobeying God and choosing to live a sinful lifestyle despite His repeated warnings?

4. Do you spend more time watching TV than you spend with your Creator?

5. Are you comfortable watching and listening to sinful behavior on TV, in movies, and on the Internet, knowing that it does not glorify God and that His Word clearly forbids it?

6. Whose side are you on: Jesus' or the world's? Whose philosophy do you subscribe to? Do you say that you love the one and actually live for the other?

7. Do you take sinning against God lightly or accept that some sins are okay?

8. Do you think God accepts our requests for forgiveness for sins we have no intention of forsaking? Do you think that's what God meant by "repent"?

9. Do you analyze how good your faith is by comparing it to others, instead of comparing it to God's Word?

10. Do you feel restless, irritable, and unfulfilled?

11. Do you feel insignificant at times?

12. Do you justify complacency in yourself as well as in others?

13. Do you defend worldliness and disobedience?

14. Is your definition of saving faith a mere acknowledgment that Jesus Christ exists; or is your definition of faith something that transcends from a mutual love relationship that manifests itself in obedience to His Word?

We were created in His image; therefore we will only find true fulfillment and stability by serving Him. We were created to be totally dependent on God in every area of our lives. To take all direction from Him and to live in obedience to His will. To live any other way is not God's intended plan. To live any other way is to live off balance and to live a fruitless unfulfilled life, opposite of God's intended purpose.

If we are not totally yielded to Jesus Christ, then we are yielding our lives to something else. We are taking directions from someone or something other then God's Word. It is impossible for any person not to be dependent on, or not to be yielding to something. People who tell you they are not dependent on, or a slave to anyone or anything, are lying to you—pride and self are their gods. If they're not a slave to Christ, they're a slave to sin. To be dependent on your own thoughts, to follow your own desires and philosophy, is the sin of idolatry and rebellion—making self a god. Those who claim they are not slaves to anything, live their lives with no restraint. They follow their own carnal desires and philosophies to which they pride themselves because they are full of self-love.

We must be careful! What the philosophies of this world believe and espouse to be right, and what is really right according to God's Word are very different. How the world thinks we should spend our day and how God wants us to spend our day are opposites. Those who do not follow God's Word and live for Him are slaves to sin. They are puppets of Satan being manipulated by him in everything they do. "Jesus answered them, I assure you, most solemnly I tell you, whoever commits and practices sin is the slave of sin" (John 8:34 AMP).

We need to remember: "the Word became flesh and dwelt among us" (John 1:14). If we are not following Jesus Christ, then we are obviously following someone else. If we are not professing that the Word of God is true and should be followed, then we are professing some other false philosophy. There is no neutral or middle ground. You either serve one or the other—Jesus Christ or Satan. At the end of this life, you either go to eternity in heaven with Christ or eternity in hell with Satan.

Do you not know that if you present yourselves to anyone as obedient slaves, you are slaves of the one whom you obey, either of sin, which leads to death, or of obedience, which leads to righteousness?

—Romans 6:16 (ESV)

*For the wages of sin is death, but the free gift of God is eternal life in
Christ Jesus our Lord.*

—Romans 6:23 (ESV)

*No servant can serve two masters, for either he will hate the one and
love the other, or he will be devoted to the one and despise the other.
You cannot serve God and money.*

—Luke 16:13 (ESV)

You cannot fully serve God if something else has all of your heart and
your attention. You have to choose a side; your loyalties can't be divided.
Otherwise you will love the one and hate the other, or you will depend on
the one and ignore the other.

We will be miserable if we are living our lives in the middle ground,
never fully giving ourselves over to either side. If we are living in this lukewarm state, our faith will be unstable and we will lack confidence in God's
Word. For part of the day we might serve our worldly lusts, and the rest of
the day might be spent trying to serve Christ—or flip—flopping back and
forth throughout the day depending on where we are and whom we are
with. What happens is that we never fully give ourselves over to worldly
lusts because of the conviction and guilt it brings and the fact we know it
is wrong. But we never fully give ourselves over to Christ either, because
deep within our hearts we secretly still want to pursue our lusts. So we are
caught in the miserable middle, the outcome of living a life opposite of the
way God intended.

God gives numerous warnings to those that live in this lukewarm state.

*I know your works: you are neither cold nor hot. Would that you
were either cold or hot! So, because you are lukewarm, and neither
hot nor cold, I will spit you out of my mouth.*

—Revelation 3:15-16 (ESV)

People who are lukewarm are worse off than those who are cold,
because they profess to be Christians and think they are serving Christ, but
in all actuality they are spiritually bankrupt and full of compromise. Those
who are cold or alienated from God know they are not living for the Lord,

they are either convicted by that fact or they don't care. Those who are hot, seek, serve, and love to obey Him in everything they do. That is why God would rather we were cold or hot than lukewarm, for when we are lukewarm we are deceived thinking that we are all right, when in reality we are not.

> *Trust in the LORD with all thine heart; and lean not unto thine own understanding. In all thy ways acknowledge him, and he shall direct thy paths. Be not wise in thine own eyes: fear the LORD, and depart from evil.*
>
> —Proverbs 3:5-7 (KJV)

We were created to be totally dependent on God for all our daily needs, for we only find fulfillment in our lives by living this way. The Bible makes it clear that God wants us to trust Him, obey Him, yield to Him, and depend upon Him daily. If we are doing those four things, we are less likely to be overcome with the daily anxieties and worries of life. With our security and stability in Christ, and not in the things of this world, we will less likely be moved by fear. We can know that no matter what happens, God is in control and has our best interests at heart.

If we are dependent on God and obedient to His Word, our faith and trust in Him will grow. Then, when major problems and trials come that are too overwhelming to handle, we will not look at the situation with our natural eyes, but through the eyes of faith. We will also look to God to solve the problem and not try to work it out in our own strength. We will not allow fear and worry to overwhelm us knowing that the situation is completely out of our hands.

We are to completely trust and obey Him in all of life's circumstances by not relying on our own wisdom and understanding. If we try to direct our own lives according to our own wisdom, we cut ourselves off from God's wisdom and direction within our lives.

> *But be doers of the word, and not hearers only, deceiving yourselves. For if anyone is a hearer of the word and not a doer, he is like a man who looks intently at his natural face in a mirror. For he looks at himself and goes away and at once forgets what he was like. But the*

one who looks into the perfect law, the law of liberty, and perseveres, being no hearer who forgets but a doer who acts, he will be blessed in his doing.

—James 1:22-25 (ESV)

For not the hearers of the law are just before God, but the doers of the law shall be justified.

—Romans 2:13 (KJV)

We can grow up attending a church every week where the minister preaches pure truth. We can even know what the Bible says inside and out and have the ability to articulate it with ease. But, if we are not living according to God's Word and doing what it says, we are deceiving ourselves. Deceived because we are only hearers of God's Word and not doers. We see this deception in many professed believers, "They profess to know God, but they deny him by their works. They are detestable, disobedient, unfit for any good work" (Titus 1:16 ESV).

In James 1 we are given an analogy of a person who does not act on what he hears: "For if anyone is a hearer of the word and not a doer, he is like a man who looks intently at his natural face in a mirror. For he looks at himself and goes away and at once forgets what he was like" (vv.23-24). The Word of God exposes our hearts and shows us areas in our lives that need to be changed. God's Word also exposes areas in our lives that are hindering us from obtaining a greater faith and intimacy in Him. So when we do not act on what we hear, it is like looking at our reflection in the mirror and seeing the flaws and dirt on our face and immediately forgetting what we have seen when we walk away.[1] We forget because we do not stay at the mirror and act upon what we are seeing in order to correct it. We never correct our flaws, so every time we go to the mirror we see the same image, nothing ever changing or being corrected.

Hearing and studying the Word of God can only benefit us if we obey and act on it. "But the one who looks into the perfect law, the law of liberty, and perseveres, being no hearer who forgets but a doer who acts, he will be blessed in his doing" (v.25). God blesses those who hear the Word of God and embrace it by persevering to carry it out. God pours out His grace to those that seek and obey Him. Through that process of living an obedient relationship with Jesus Christ, we are transformed and our faith will grow.

Using the example of the mirror, when we see a blemish on our face, we should look closer and examine it, and then we should work to fix it.[2] Just as when we hear God's Word and are convicted by it, we should embrace it instead of resisting and rejecting it. By embracing God's Word and the conviction of the Holy Spirit, we allow the truth to dispel the lies in our lives. This conviction is good because it helps keep us from being deceived and keeps us vigilant in our pursuit of God's transformation in those areas. When we persevere in our pursuit to know Jesus Christ, we will naturally obey Him and be given the grace and ability to be a doer of the Word. The more we pursue Him, the deeper our faith will grow, and as our faith grows we have more confidence in His Word. The more faith and confidence we have in His Word, the more we will believe and act upon it.

The result of having a deeper faith is not allowing any doubt, unbelief, or fear to get in the way of our relationship with Jesus Christ. We trust Him no matter what things look like in the natural. To have faith means that we believe God's Word, so therefore we obey it. An obedient faith produces holiness and the power to overcome the many temptations that come upon us daily. This faith does not fall for Satan's lies, lies that would cause us to disobey and doubt God, and does not allow anyone or anything to neuter, hinder, or distract us from pursuing God's perfect will.

> *The thief cometh not, but for to steal, and to kill, and to destroy: I am come that they might have life, and that they might have it more abundantly.*
>
> —John 10:10 (KJV)

It is very important to have a daily discipline of prayer and the study of God's Word. We need to be continually filling our lives with truth. This is something we can't slack on or blow off. If we are not serious about seeking the Lord daily, we're allowing our own thoughts, or the world's philosophies, to have dominion in our lives. Then we leave ourselves vulnerable to the temptations of sin and the lies of Satan. Satan's tactic is to get us to doubt God's Word so we will disobey it. Satan causes us to think it's better to follow our own desires than to obey God; to get us to not take seriously the warnings and consequences of disobeying God's Word. This is the same tactic Satan has used throughout history starting in the Garden of Eden.

When God formed Adam, He put him in the Garden of Eden to live. This garden had an abundance of fruit trees and plants that would supply all of Adam's needs. He would not lack for anything. God gave Adam the task of taking care of His creation (garden), working under God's direction. The Lord told Adam he could eat from every tree of the garden, "but of the tree of the knowledge of good and evil you shall not eat, for in the day that you eat of it you shall surely die" (Gen 2:17 ESV).

Adam had an unhindered love relationship with God in the garden. God showed His love to Adam by creating him and taking care of his every need. Adam willingly obeyed God because of the love God was showing him. As long as Adam obeyed God, he would enjoy this perfect relationship for all of eternity.

But God had created man with a choice to obey Him. When God placed Adam in the garden, He gave him dominion over all the animals and told him he could eat from every tree except for one. For if he ate from the "tree of the knowledge of good and evil," his disobedience of God's command would cause death.

God saw that it was not good that Adam was alone; he needed a companion suited for him, one who would help him fulfill God's will in his life. So God created Eve for him. God made a woman especially suited for Adam out of one of his ribs. She was an equal companion who would help him fulfill God's will in his life. Adam and Eve were bound to God by their absolute faith and trust in Him. They believed God and obeyed Him by taking all direction from Him. Satan, who is an enemy of God and of anyone who is aligned with God, knew this and wanted to cause division between God and the people He had created.

So Satan set out to tempt Adam and Eve by causing them to doubt and not believe what God had told them. He did this by masquerading as a serpent and questioning Eve about what God had told her. Eve told Satan that they could eat from every tree in the garden except for "the tree of the knowledge of good and evil" (Gen. 2:17), because God told them, "Ye shall not eat of it, neither shall ye touch it, lest ye die" (Gen. 3:3).

> *And the serpent said unto the woman, ye shall not surely die: For God doth know that in the day ye eat thereof, then your eyes shall be opened, and ye shall be as gods, knowing good and evil. And when the woman saw that the tree was good for food, and that it was pleasant to the eyes, and a tree to be desired to make one wise, she took the fruit thereof, and did eat, and gave also unto her husband with her; and he did eat.*
>
> —Genesis 3:4-6

Satan lied to them by contradicting what God had told them; by telling them they would not die if they ate the fruit from the forbidden tree. Satan made it sound like they would be better off if they disobeyed God, because their "eyes shall be opened, and ye shall be as gods, knowing good and evil." Satan got them to doubt and question the truth of what God had told them. He was able to get their eyes and thoughts off God and their eyes and thoughts on the forbidden fruit. They lusted after the forbidden fruit because it looked good and they wanted to taste it, plus they desired the wisdom that the tree offered. Satan told them they would be like gods, "knowing good and evil." They would be able to decide for themselves what was good or evil. They would be able to live independently from God's Word and make up their own morals and standards to live by derived from their own hearts. Satan enticed them into thinking that they would be gods of their own lives. It was a complete lie that still infects our society today! We were created to live our lives for Jesus Christ and obey God's Word. Only God can determine what is good or evil in society and in our lives.

That's exactly what Satan tries to do in our lives. He lies to us by trying to get us to doubt the truth of God's Word. He blurs our thinking to make us believe that God does not mean what He says. He causes us to disregard the warnings God has given us in His Word and to live however we deem right. Satan blinds us to the truth that there is a judgment for sin.

He blinds us to the fact that salvation and righteousness is only found in Jesus Christ. He tempts us to reject or not take seriously our relationship with Jesus Christ, a relationship that would give us the forgiveness of sins and the power to live a sanctified life. Satan wants us to reject the truth and believe our own self-generated lie.

That is exactly what is happening today; we are thinking, and behaving as if we were gods. We are rejecting God's revealed truth and are operating independent of Him. From the beginning of creation, God determined what is right and wrong, and He revealed it to us in His Word. But people in our society are coming up with their own morals and standards, derived from their own minds, contrary to God's Word and what He has written in our hearts (Rom. 1:18-20). They are not consulting God and His Word as their source and are rejecting how God has told us to live. When we sin against God by rejecting Him, we bring death on ourselves. What kind of death? Separation from God, which if not repented of will lead to eternity in hell.

Satan got Adam and Eve to reject God's truth and believe the age-old lie that doing your own thing will bring fulfillment. They took their eyes off God and focused their eyes on the forbidden fruit, which they lusted after (Gen. 3:6). As soon as they ate the fruit, they brought spiritual death to their lives, because their relationship with God was destroyed. They no longer could have that close communion they once had with God in the garden.

Because of Adam and Eve's disobedience, they would experience physical death. They would grow old and die. Their disobedience caused sin to enter into the world and brought death to all mankind, because everyone from that point on would be born with a sin nature. Adam and Eve brought corruption into their own hearts, which resulted in all of mankind being born with a corrupted nature (an impulse to sin). The result of sin is death; therefore, because everyone has sinned, everyone will experience death. The result of all this was that God kicked them out of the garden (His presence), because God is holy and no one can stand before God if they are not holy (without sin).

Wherefore, as by one man sin entered into the world, and death by sin; and so death passed upon all men, for that all have sinned.

—Romans 5:12

Adam and Eve's relationship with God in the Garden of Eden was severed through their disobedience, which resulted in them being kicked out of the garden (His presence). Now their relationship with God would be totally different from what they had before.

They would now be dependent on God through inward and outward trials, as well as hardships that they would not have experienced in the garden.

When they ate the forbidden fruit, their eyes were opened and they "knew that they were naked," and they became ashamed (Gen. 3:7-11). Before they disobeyed God, they were morally pure and innocent in everything they thought or did, because they did not have a corrupted heart. After they sinned, corruption came into their hearts, and they were sinful and ashamed. Because of the sin that nakedness would bring into the world, God made "coats of skins, and clothed them" (Gen. 3:21). From the very start, God showed us the severity of sinning against Him. He also showed us the blessings that come with obedience.

Even though sin entered into the world and separated everyone from God, God still loved the people He created and desired a meaningful relationship. So God, in order to teach the severity of sin and the blessings that come with obedience, instituted a number of laws for the people to follow. These laws would convict the people of their sin and show them the consequences of their disobedience. The law showed them that they could not follow all these laws and ordinances in their own strength. Most of all, it showed the people they needed a Redeemer to redeem them from their sins and a Mediator to mediate for them before God.

For the life of the flesh is in the blood: and I have given it to you upon the altar to make atonement for your souls: for it is the blood that maketh an atonement for the soul.

—Leviticus 17:11

In the Old Testament, the only atonement for sin was the shedding of blood. God instituted this by shedding blood for animal skins to cover Adam and Eve's nakedness, sin (Gen. 3:21). Only by the shedding of blood could atonement be made for sin. It could not purge their conscience from guilt or free them from the bondage that sin brought. It was to prepare the people for Jesus to come as their mediator and the perfect sacrifice for their sins.

Sin was very costly; you could only sacrifice the best animals, which otherwise could have been eaten or sold. God is holy and righteous and nothing that is unholy can stand before Him. So the people could only come before God with their animal sacrifices to atone for their sins. The only atonement for sin that God would accept is the shedding of blood; "without the shedding of blood there is no forgiveness of sins" (Heb. 9:22 ESV). Following the law with its sacrifices taught the people how to be obedient to God and outlined the consequences of disobedience.

The laws and sacrifices prepared the people for the coming Messiah. This coming Messiah would fulfill the prophecies concerning Him and would become their perfect sacrifice. All the prophecies concerning the Messiah were fulfilled in the coming of Jesus Christ.

Jesus became our perfect sacrifice, fulfilling all of God's righteous standards by being in complete obedience to Him. He obeyed the law both outwardly and inwardly, perfectly without sin. Jesus took our sin, our punishment for sin, by being crucified on the cross. There is no longer a need for any more sacrifices; Jesus fulfilled that requirement. Now everyone can come to God through faith in Jesus Christ, not standing on his or her own righteousness, but on the righteousness of Christ. Through Jesus Christ, we have forgiveness of sin, the purging of our conscience of guilt, and the power to overcome sin and bondage in our lives.

That is why it's so important that we take serious what God has commanded us in His Word by studying it, obeying it, and applying these truths to our lives. One of the main aspects of being able to hear and apply the truth is getting rid of the sin and evil influences that would hinder it. Those evil influences can be the places we go to or the friends we hang out with. They can also be what we are listening to or reading. Everything we are involved in is either drawing us closer to Christ, which means we are growing in faith, or pushing us away. If we allow these evil influences to infiltrate our lives, they will have a natural tendency to water down or cause us not to take the Word of God seriously. When we don't take the Word of God seriously, we obviously won't obey it. That is why merely hearing the Word of God is meaningless if not acted upon. God does not accept disobedience, lukewarmness, or mere intellectual knowledge. Those who act upon what they hear and obey it are the only ones accepted by God.

"My mother and my brothers are those who hear the word of God and do it."

—Luke 8:21 (ESV)

CHAPTER 9

▼

WHAT YOU MEANT FOR
EVIL, GOD MEANT FOR
GOOD

When he summoned a famine on the land and broke all supply of bread, he had sent a man ahead of them, Joseph, who was sold as a slave. His feet were hurt with fetters; his neck was put in a collar of iron; until what he had said came to pass, the word of the LORD tested him. The king sent and released him; the ruler of the peoples set him free; he made him lord of his house and ruler of all his possessions, to bind his princes at his pleasure and to teach his elders wisdom. Then Israel came to Egypt; Jacob sojourned in the land of Ham. And the LORD made his people very fruitful and made them stronger than their foes.

—Psalm 105:16-24 (ESV)

Jacob lived in the land of Canaan with his three remaining wives and 12 sons. Rachel had been the only wife he truly loved, and the other three were forced upon him. Jacob's father-in-law had tricked him into marrying Rachel's older sister, Leah. Leah bore Jacob six sons: Reuben, Simeon, Levi, Judah, Issachar, and Zebulun. Bilhah was Rachel's handmaid given to Jacob because she was barren. She bore Dan and Naphtali. Leah also gave her handmaid Zilpah to Jacob to have surrogate children by her. She bore Gad and Asher. Jacob's beloved Rachel was the last to conceive. She bore a son named Joseph, her firstborn. She later died on her way to the land of Canaan while giving birth to Benjamin, Joseph's younger brother. Jacob loved Rachel and missed her very much, and the only remembrance of his beautiful wife was her two sons, Joseph and Benjamin.

Jacob loved Joseph above all of his other sons because he was the first-born son of his favored wife Rachel. Joseph was younger than all of his other brothers except Benjamin, but he proved to be more trustworthy than all the rest. Jacob probably did not trust his other sons and showed open partiality to Joseph.

When Joseph was 17 years old, he pastured a flock with his brothers, the sons of Bilhah and Zilpah. When they arrived back home, "Joseph brought a bad report of them to their father" (Gen. 37:2 ESV). Joseph probably reported his brother's misconducts. The Bible is silent on what their misconduct might have been; nevertheless, it added fuel to the tension that already existed between Joseph and his brothers because he was favored.

> *Israel loved Joseph more than any other of his sons, because he was the son of his old age. And he made him a robe of many colors. But when his brothers saw that their father loved him more than all his brothers, they hated him and could not speak peacefully to him. Now Joseph had a dream, and when he told it to his brothers they hated him even more. He said to them, "Hear this dream that I have dreamed: Behold, we were binding sheaves in the field, and behold, my sheaf arose and stood upright. And behold, your sheaves gathered around it and bowed down to my sheaf."*
>
> —Genesis 37:3-7 (ESV)

Jacob gave Joseph a robe made up of many different colors, which was a sign of distinction and favoritism. Jacob might have been planning to make Joseph his successor instead of his other sons. Reuben, who was the firstborn and natural heir to the birthright, was disqualified because he had sex with Bilhah, one of his father's concubines (Gen. 35:22). The next two in succession for the birthright were Simeon and Levi, who were disqualified because of the ruthless crimes they committed in Shechem (Gen. 34:25-30). This left Judah, the fourth in the natural birthright order.[1] Nevertheless, it is implied that Jacob wanted his son Joseph to be heir to the birthright.

Instead of Joseph keeping the dream he had received from the Lord to himself, he added more fuel to the fire by telling his brothers about it. This dream was easy for his brothers to discern and understand. They would one day bow down and pay homage to Joseph. His brothers responded by saying, "'Are you indeed to reign over us? Or are you indeed to rule over us?' So they hated him even more for his dreams and for his words" (Gen 37:8 ESV). Then Joseph dreamed yet another dream and told his brothers. Joseph dreamed that the sun, moon, and 11 stars were bowing down to him.

> But when he told it to his father and to his brothers, his father rebuked him and said to him, "What is this dream that you have dreamed? Shall I and your mother and your brothers indeed come to bow ourselves to the ground before you?" And his brothers were jealous of him, but his father kept the saying in mind.
>
> —Genesis 37:10-11 (ESV)

Jacob publicly rebuked Joseph in front of his brothers, most likely to cool down the situation. By publicly rebuking Joseph, it might have satisfied the brothers' anger for a season by showing a division between Jacob and his favored son. By rebuking Joseph, he could show that he was not encouraging Joseph or in agreement with his dream. But the text tells us that Jacob "kept the saying in mind." Jacob thought about the dreams that Joseph had, and kept them in his heart and remembered them till they came to pass. The immediate situation warranted a rebuke, but there was something about Joseph's dreams that Jacob believed deep within.

Joseph's brothers went to pasture their father's sheep near the town of Shechem. Joseph stayed back with his father while his brothers took the sheep out to pasture. Jacob probably thought the time separated from each other would help heal the tension between them. After they had been there awhile, Jacob decided to send Joseph to check out how his brothers and the flock were doing and then to return with the news. So he sent Joseph from the Valley of Hebron to Shechem to find his brothers to check on them. When Joseph arrived in Shechem, a man who lived there told him his brothers had taken the flock to Dothan. So he set out to find them.

> *They saw him from afar, and before he came near to them they con-*
> *spired against him to kill him. They said to one another, "Here*
> *comes this dreamer. Come now, let us kill him and throw him into*
> *one of the pits. Then we will say that a fierce animal has devoured*
> *him, and we will see what will become of his dreams." But when*
> *Reuben heard it, he rescued him out of their hands, saying, "Let us*
> *not take his life." And Reuben said to them, "Shed no blood; cast*
> *him into this pit here in the wilderness, but do not lay a hand on*
> *him"—that he might rescue him out of their hand to restore him to*
> *his father. So when Joseph came to his brothers, they stripped him of*
> *his robe, the robe of many colors that he wore. And they took him*
> *and cast him into a pit. The pit was empty; there was no water in it.*
>
> —Genesis 37:18-24 (ESV)

When they saw Joseph coming to them from a distance, they decided they were going to kill him. They wanted to kill him and throw his body into one of the pits and tell their father that a wild animal had devoured him. They were unified in their hatred for Joseph. They didn't just hate him for the favoritism he received from Jacob their father, nor the dreams that he had told them about; underlying it all was something else. They most likely could not stand being around Joseph because of his upright character and integrity. They were convicted by his presence and uncomfortable around him—they wanted to get rid of him for good!

Reuben, the firstborn, was the only one who stood up to stop Joseph from being killed. He told his brothers: "Let us not take his life." He suggested throwing him into the pit instead. Reuben secretly wanted to come back and deliver Joseph and personally take him back to his father. Reuben most likely wanted to deliver Joseph to his father in order to win back the favor he had lost due to his sexual indiscretion with Bilhah. If Reuben truly cared for Joseph, he would have tried to secure his release right away, but he didn't. Instead of warning Joseph or stopping the brothers from harming him, Reuben suggested throwing him into the pit instead so that he could deceive his brothers into thinking he was with them, when he surely wasn't. He had his own agenda in mind, which was probably to win back his birthright and his father's favor.

When Joseph arrived at his brother's location, they stripped him of his "robe of many colors" and threw him into the pit. Then the brothers sat down to eat. While they were eating, a caravan of Midianite traders from Gilead approached. They were on their way to Egypt to trade their goods. Judah suggested that they sell Joseph to the Midianites instead of killing him "for he is our brother, our own flesh." The Midianite traders were known for trafficking slaves to Egypt. The brothers agreed with Judah, drew Joseph out of the pit, and sold him to the traders.

Reuben was not there when his brothers sold Joseph into slavery. When he returned to the pit and saw that Joseph was not there, he tore his clothes and was worried that as the firstborn he would be held responsible. Reuben had thought to win his father's favor, but instead he would be in greater trouble for allowing this to happen.

> *Then they took Joseph's robe and slaughtered a goat and dipped the robe in the blood. And they sent the robe of many colors and brought it to their father and said, "This we have found; please identify whether it is your son's robe or not." And he identified it and said, "It is my son's robe. A fierce animal has devoured him. Joseph is without doubt torn to pieces." Then Jacob tore his garments and put sackcloth on his loins and mourned for his son many days. All his sons and all his daughters rose up to comfort him, but he refused to be comforted and said, "No, I shall go down to Sheol to my son, mourning." Thus his father wept for him. Meanwhile the Midianites had sold him in Egypt to Potiphar, an officer of Pharaoh, the captain of the guard.*
>
> —Genesis 37:31-36 (ESV)

The brothers deceived their father by dipping Joseph's robe of many colors in goat's blood and causing Jacob to believe a wild animal killed Joseph. Upon hearing the news of his son, Jacob went into mourning for many days and would not be comforted. He missed his son Joseph and wept for him.

Joseph was brought to Egypt and sold to Potiphar, an officer of Pharaoh, the captain of the guard. At this point, Joseph must have felt very betrayed by his brothers, scared, and lonely. He went from being a favored son to being tied up and taken to Egypt to be sold as a slave. Nevertheless, he did not allow bitterness, betrayal, and anger to affect his faithfulness to God. From the very start, he was successful, because God was with him.

"His master saw that the LORD was with him and that the LORD caused all that he did to succeed in his hands. So Joseph found favor in his sight and attended him, and he made him overseer of his house and put him in charge of all that he had" (Gen. 39:3-4 ESV).

The Lord blessed Potiphar's house and all his fields for Joseph's sake. So he put Joseph in charge of everything he owned and did not have to worry about a thing.

After he had been there awhile, his master's wife lusted after Joseph and wanted him to "lie with her." Joseph refused her advances and told her that his master had put him in charge of everything and had not withheld anything "except yourself, because you are his wife. How then can I do this great wickedness and sin against God?" (v.9). Joseph was loyal and would not betray his master, but most of all he would not sin against God, which was his greater concern. We can see that from a very young age Joseph had a very strong relationship with the Lord. He was first and foremost obedient to the Lord, and he knew that the Lord prospered him because of that. Even in the midst of all the bad things that had happened to him, he knew the Lord was with him every step of the way.

Day after day, the master's wife pestered Joseph "to lie beside her or to be with her," but Joseph would not succumb to her.

And as she spoke to Joseph day after day, he would not listen to her, to lie beside her or to be with her. But one day, when he went into the house to do his work and none of the men of the house was there in the house, she caught him by his garment, saying, "Lie with me." But he left his garment in her hand and fled and got out of the house. And as soon as she saw that he had left his garment in her hand and

had fled out of the house, she called to the men of her household and
said to them, "See, he has brought among us a Hebrew to laugh at
us. He came in to me to lie with me, and I cried out with a loud
voice. And as soon as he heard that I lifted up my voice and cried
out, he left his garment beside me and fled and got out of the house."
—Genesis 39:10-15 (ESV)

One day when no one was around the house but Joseph, the master's wife took advantage of the situation and grabbed Joseph by his garment and wanted to him to "lie with her." But Joseph refused her advances and fled the scene leaving his garment behind in her hand. The master's wife got so angry with Joseph for refusing her request that she fabricated a story that Joseph had tried to force her to "lie" with him. When the master of the house heard his wife's story, he sent Joseph to prison, the prison where the king's prisoners were confined.

But the Lord worked mightily in Joseph's life while he was there and gave him favor with the keeper of the prison. The keeper of the prison saw how faithful and wise Joseph was in everything he did, so he put him in charge of all the prisoners and the daily business of running the prison. "And whatever he did, the LORD made it succeed" (v.23).

Pharaoh, the king of Egypt, was angry with two of his officers, his cupbearer and his baker, so he committed them to prison. The captain of the guard appointed Joseph to attend to them. One night they both had a dream while they slept and woke up disturbed because they didn't have anyone who could interpret their dreams. "And Joseph said to them, "Do not interpretations belong to God? Please tell them to me" (Gen. 40:8 ESV).

So the cupbearer and the baker told Joseph their dreams. Joseph interpreted their dreams accurately, for they both came to pass. Pharaoh restored the chief cupbearer to his former position, but hanged the chief baker, just as Joseph had interpreted. Before Pharaoh had restored the chief cupbearer to his former position, Joseph told him: "Only remember me, when it is well with you, and please do me the kindness to mention me to Pharaoh, and so get me out of this house. For I was indeed stolen out of the land of the Hebrews, and here also I have done nothing that they should put me into the pit" (Gen. 40:14 ESV). Joseph wanted the cupbearer to help him get out of prison, but when the cupbearer was released he forgot about Joseph.

Two years later, Pharaoh had a dream. In the dream he stood by the Nile River and watched as seven healthy and attractive cows come out of the river to eat grass. Then, as he was watching, seven thin and ugly cows came up out of the Nile River and ate the seven healthy cows. Then Pharaoh woke up. When he went back to sleep, he dreamed a second time. In this dream, he saw seven good ears of corn growing on one stalk. Then he saw seven ears of corn that were thin and withering. The seven thin ears swallowed up the seven good ears.

In the morning, Pharaoh was very troubled by his dreams, so he called in all the wise men and magicians of Egypt to hear his dreams and give him an interpretation. But none of the wise men or magicians were able to interpret his dreams. Then the chief cupbearer remembered how Joseph had interpreted his and the chief baker's dreams while they were in prison. So he told Pharaoh about how Joseph had accurately interpreted their dreams and that both interpretations had come to pass.

Upon hearing the news, Pharaoh sent for Joseph. "And Pharaoh said to Joseph, 'I have had a dream, and there is no one who can interpret it. I have heard it said of you that when you hear a dream you can interpret it.' Joseph answered Pharaoh, 'It is not in me; God will give Pharaoh a favorable answer'" (Gen. 41:15-16 ESV).

Pharaoh told Joseph his dreams, and Joseph was able to interpret them. Joseph gave all the glory to God and took none of the credit for himself. Pharaoh and all the people could see that God was with Joseph and had given him great wisdom and discernment.

Joseph told Pharaoh that both of the dreams had one meaning. "The seven good cows are seven years, and the seven good ears are seven years; the dreams are one. The seven lean and ugly cows that came up after them are seven years, and the seven empty ears blighted by the east wind are also seven years of famine" (vv.26-27). Joseph told Pharaoh that God was telling him what was about to happen in the land. There would be seven years of bountiful harvests throughout Egypt, but after that there would be seven years of extreme famine. The famine would be so extreme and severe that the people would forget what it was like to have plenty. God gave Pharaoh the dream twice to show that these seven years of plenty and the seven years of famine were fixed by God and would come to pass. Then Joseph said to Pharaoh:

> *Now therefore let Pharaoh select a discerning and wise man, and set him over the land of Egypt. Let Pharaoh proceed to appoint overseers over the land and take one-fifth of the produce of the land of Egypt during the seven plentiful years. And let them gather all the food of these good years that are coming and store up grain under the authority of Pharaoh for food in the cities, and let them keep it. That food shall be a reserve for the land against the seven years of famine that are to occur in the land of Egypt, so that the land may not perish through the famine."*
>
> —Genesis 41:33-36 (ESV)

Joseph was given such wisdom and insight from God into the problem Egypt was about to face, that he instructed the Pharaoh on how to prepare for the upcoming famine. He believed Joseph's interpretation and was pleased with his proposal on how to prepare for the famine. Pharaoh was so pleased with Joseph that he said, "Since God has shown you all this, there is none so discerning and wise as you are. You shall be over my house, and all my people shall order themselves as you command" (vv.39-40).

Joseph was 30 years old when Pharaoh put him in charge of preparing Egypt for the famine. Joseph had total authority over all the people and the land in Egypt; there was no one higher in authority to Joseph than Pharaoh. Joseph had moved from being the favored son of Jacob, to being a slave, to being a prisoner, to becoming the second-in-command in Egypt. He came to Egypt when he was 17 years old; now 13 years later he was the second most powerful man in Egypt.

For seven years, the land produced abundantly and the food was stored throughout the land. Joseph had stored so much grain that it no longer could be measured. It was like "the sand of the sea" (v.49). Before the first year of the famine, two sons had been born to him. The name of the firstborn was Manasseh. "For God has made me forget all my hardship and all my father's house" (v.51). He named his second son Ephraim, "For God has made me fruitful in the land of my affliction" (v.52). Even though he had many trials and afflictions in Egypt, he enjoyed the temporal pleasures of having a family and the fact that God had made him fruitful despite everything that had happened. He knew, without a shadow of a doubt, that the Lord was the one who made him prosperous in the land of his captivity. By now Joseph realized that God had allowed and orchestrated everything that happened to him for a divine purpose—to preserve life.

> *The seven years of plenty that occurred in the land of Egypt came to an end, and the seven years of famine began to come, as Joseph had said. There was famine in all lands, but in all the land of Egypt there was bread. When all the land of Egypt was famished, the people cried to Pharaoh for bread. Pharaoh said to all the Egyptians, "Go to Joseph. What he says to you, do." So when the famine had spread over all the land, Joseph opened all the storehouses and sold to the Egyptians, for the famine was severe in the land of Egypt. Moreover, all the earth came to Egypt to Joseph to buy grain, because the famine was severe over all the earth.*
>
> —Genesis 41:53-57 (ESV)

The famine had spread throughout Egypt and the surrounding nations including the land of Canaan where his father and brothers lived. The Egyptians were the only ones who had stored up food and grain to prepare for this famine, because of Joseph. So when the people from the surrounding nations ran out of food, they went to Egypt to buy food from Joseph.

Jacob heard that Egypt had food, so he sent 10 of Joseph's brothers to Egypt to buy food. He did not send Joseph's younger brother, Benjamin, because he was afraid something bad might happen to him on the trip. So Joseph's brothers came to Egypt and bowed down to Joseph. Joseph recognized his brothers but they did not recognize him. This was probably due to the fact that Joseph was a young man when he went to Egypt. Now it was over 20 years later, plus Joseph looked, dressed, and spoke like an Egyptian. Joseph probably recognized them because there were 10 of them, plus they came from Canaan dressed as they usually did from that area.

Joseph remembered the dreams the Lord had given him where his brothers bowed down to him, and now it was being fulfilled before his eyes. Joseph took them through a series of tests to find out about his family and to humble them in order to see how sincere their hearts were. He wanted to find out if they were grieved over selling him into slavery. Joseph spoke to them through an interpreter and did not reveal to them that he knew them or understood their language.

First he accused them of being spies and put them in prison for three days. Then he released all of them except for Simeon and sent them home with enough food for their families. He told them if they wanted Simeon released and wanted more food, they had to prove they were not spies by bringing back Benjamin. When the brothers heard what Joseph had said, "they said to one another, 'In truth we are guilty concerning our brother, in that we saw the distress of his soul, when he begged us and we did not listen. That is why this distress has come upon us.' And Reuben answered them, 'Did I not tell you not to sin against the boy? But you did not listen. So now there comes a reckoning for his blood'" (Gen. 42:21-22 ESV). While they were talking, they did not know that Joseph was listening and understood their conversation. After Joseph heard what they had said, he turned away and wept secretly. When he returned, he had Simeon bound before their eyes and sent them on their way.

They eventually ran out of the food they had brought back from Egypt and were desperate. So Jacob was forced to send Joseph's brothers back with Benjamin to Egypt to obtain more food. This time Joseph had his steward bring all his brothers into his house for a banquet dinner where he honored Benjamin with a portion of food that was five times greater than the others. They were then sent away with the food needed to sustain their families, but Joseph had the steward put his silver cup in Benjamin's sack. When they had gone a short distance from the city, Joseph sent his steward after them to catch them for stealing his cup. After the steward searched all the brothers' grain sacks, he found the silver cup in Benjamin's sack. When the brothers were brought back to Joseph's house, they bowed down to him and tried to clear up the matter. Joseph told them that because Benjamin stole his cup, he belonged to Joseph and would be his servant, but the rest could go home. Judah stood and spoke for his brothers and tried to persuade Joseph to change his mind. This same Judah, who had talked his brothers into selling Joseph into slavery, was willing to sacrifice his life for Benjamin's release. Judah said to Joseph: "Now therefore, please let your servant remain instead of the boy as a servant to my lord, and let the boy go back with his brothers. For how can I go back to my father if the boy is not with me? I fear to see the evil that would find my father" (Gen. 44:33-34 ESV).

Upon hearing that Judah was willing to take the punishment for his brother, Joseph could contain himself no more. He broke down into tears and revealed himself to them. He hugged every one of his brothers, showing how much he loved and had truly forgiven them.

> "I am your brother, Joseph, whom you sold into Egypt. And now do not be distressed or angry with yourselves because you sold me here, for God sent me before you to preserve life. For the famine has been in the land these two years, and there are yet five years in which there will be neither plowing nor harvest. And God sent me before you to preserve for you a remnant on earth, and to keep alive for you many survivors. So it was not you who sent me here, but God. He has made me a father to Pharaoh, and lord of all his house and ruler over all the land of Egypt.
>
> —Genesis 45:4-8 (ESV)

Joseph told them to not be bothered by the fact that they had sold him into slavery; he knew that God sent him there to preserve life. Joseph told his brothers that God sent him there to "preserve for you a remnant," to keep alive God's chosen people. He told them that because there were still five years left in the famine, in order to survive they needed to go back and get their father Jacob and all their families. They could come to Egypt and settle in the land of Goshen near Joseph. In Goshen, they would be able to remain separate from the Egyptians, and Joseph could easily supply them and their families with food so that they would survive.

Joseph's brothers returned to the land of Canaan and brought back Jacob and their families. They settled in the Land of Goshen—a total of 70 people including Joseph (Exod. 1:5). Jacob was reunited with Joseph and was comforted in his old age. Before Jacob died, he blessed Joseph and his two sons and gave them a portion of the inheritance in the land of Canaan. He told Joseph about God's promise to him: "Behold, I will make you fruitful and multiply you, and I will make of you a company of peoples and will give this land to your offspring after you for an everlasting possession" (Gen. 48:4 ESV). Jacob made Joseph swear that he would bury him in the land of Canaan (the Promised Land), not in Egypt.

After the death of Jacob, Joseph's brothers were worried that Joseph would seek revenge on them for what they had done to him, now that their father was dead. So they sent a message to Joseph asking for forgiveness. Joseph's response to his brothers shows that Joseph knew how the sovereign God had worked in his life.

> *But Joseph said to them, "Do not fear, for am I in the place of God? As for you, you meant evil against me, but God meant it for good, to bring it about that many people should be kept alive, as they are today. So do not fear; I will provide for you and your little ones." Thus he comforted them and spoke kindly to them.*
>
> —Genesis 50:19-21

Then Joseph died in Egypt, but before he died he made the sons of Jacob swear to take his body with them when God brought them back to the land of Canaan. "And Joseph said to his brothers, 'I am about to die, but God will visit you and bring you up out of this land to the land that he swore to Abraham, to Isaac, and to Jacob'" (Gen. 50:24).

Four hundred and thirty years later in the land of Egypt, the promise God gave to Abraham was fulfilled. "I will make of you a great nation, and I will bless you and make your name great, so that you will be a blessing. I will bless those who bless you, and him who dishonors you I will curse, and in you all the families of the earth shall be blessed" (Gen. 12:2-3). "I will surely bless you, and I will surely multiply your offspring as the stars of heaven and as the sand that is on the seashore" (22:17).

Only 70 people came to Egypt from the offspring of Abraham, Isaac, and Jacob. But 430 years later those 70 people had multiplied to over two million people[2] counting women and children. When Moses brought the children of Israel out of Egypt to take them to the Promised Land, they had grown into a mighty nation.

Joseph's life and everything that happened to him was an integral part of God's sovereign plan, just as our lives are a part of that plan. Joseph suffered and may have questioned God about why he was going through so much hardship and seeming punishment. Joseph certainly did not know God's overall plans. But we can see from his life that he did not allow bitterness or anger to take root and influence his relationship with the Lord or his outward faithfulness and testimony.

When Joseph became a slave, he did not know that God was going to deliver his people through him. Even so, he was faithful in the little things (Luke 16:10). He was honest, hardworking, and faithful in everything that he did. God blessed him and used him because of that, and everyone around Joseph knew that. God was preparing Joseph by humbling him and causing him not to trust in his own talents and strength but in God's—to trust in God no matter what things look like, for He is in complete control.

Joseph learned that you can't analyze what is going to happen to you in the future by analyzing your current situation. Joseph didn't allow bitterness, anger, and unforgiveness to affect his faithfulness to God or to bring dishonor to Him. Joseph probably struggled with unbelief, anger, unforgiveness, and loneliness, but he worked through those things and in the end never allowed them to take root in his life. He learned that any evil that people might do to you, God is allowing for some reason. Because of that, he had no excuse to sin against God by getting angry with his brothers or with God or to harbor unforgiveness or revenge. Most of all, Joseph learned by experience that God works all things out in our lives for our good and His glory, no matter what!

> *We know that for those who love God all things work together for good, for those who are called according to his purpose.*
>
> —Romans 8:28 (ESV)

What have we learned from Joseph's life?

1. Just because things are not going our way does not mean they're not going God's way.

2. We can't determine our future by analyzing our present.

3. God is with us every step of the way, even in our darkest hour and greatest trials.

4. No matter what evil people bring upon us, it does not give us the right to do the same to them.

5. No matter how rough our lives are or how bad our situation is, those things do not give us the excuse to disobey and sin against God.

6. If we dwell too much on the future, we will miss the opportunities that God has given us today to glorify Him.

7. God is glorified and blesses us in our daily obedience to Him.

8. Everything that we encounter in life, whether good or bad, God has allowed for His purpose.

9. Our Sovereign God has a plan for our lives and is working it all out according to His will.

10. We need to live our daily lives totally faithful and dependent on the Lord.

Faith is the substance of things hoped for, the evidence of things not seen.

—Hebrews 11:1

Conclusion

Those who know your name put their trust in you, for you, O LORD,
have not forsaken those who seek you.

—Psalm 9:10 (ESV)

True faith is believing and acting upon God's word.

When we do not understand the character and faithfulness of God, it will cause many hindrances to our walk of faith. One of the biggest hindrances we face is not knowing God and understanding His ways, which will cause us to be disobedient. We can't expect God to work in our lives if we are resisting Him. Joseph sought God and obeyed Him daily throughout his life. He obeyed and trusted God, whether he was a prisoner or Pharaoh's right-hand man. His position, status, or condition did not affect his trusting and obeying God. Because Joseph was faithful in the little things, he was given greater things. God gave him favor and wisdom and catapulted him to the top.

It is futile and makes no sense for us to pray for God's direction and will for some great decision or event in the future, if we are not living in daily obedience to Him. If we are not walking in obedience today, then most likely we will not be walking in obedience if our prayer is answered. It is total arrogance to think that we will do great things for God in the future, if we are not living for Him today. First we need to turn from our sin and yield over our lives to Him in obedience. We need to seek Him daily and allow Him to direct our lives according to His will.

If our lives are dedicated to serving Jesus Christ, we should never second-guess or doubt His presence in our lives. We cannot analyze any situation with the natural eye! We must come and seek God and look at the situation through the eyes of faith, according to the promises of God. When things are not going our way or we are having a rough time, it does not mean that God is not pleased with us or that He has turned His back on us. We should never judge or analyze our situation according to our natural mind, worldly opinion, what we think should happen, or what we want to happen. For God is working all things out in our lives for His glory and our good! "He that spared not his own Son, but delivered him up for us all, how shall he not with him also freely give us all things?" (Rom. 8:32)

I hunger for your grace to lead me through
in a world that is unlike you
to escape a chaotic world that will not last
awaiting the heavenly triumph that will erase the past.

For we walk by faith, not by sight.

—2 Corinthians 5:7

Notes

Chapter 1

1. *New Strong's Exhaustive Concordance of the Bible*, © 1990 by Thomas Nelson Publishers; 1 Peter 1:7, *trial;* concordance Greek word # 1383.

2. *Foxe's Book of Martyrs*, chap. 1, "History of Christian Martyrs to the First General Persecutions Under Nero," (Grand Rapids: Zondervan, 1967)

3. *Parallel Bible Commentary* (Nashville: Thomas Nelson, 1994), Matthew 26:36-39, Gethsemane "Olive Press," p. 1954.

4. *Unger's Concise Bible Dictionary* (Grand Rapids: Baker Book House, 1985), Definition of "Olive Dresser" p. 138.

Chapter 2

1. *Halley's Bible Handbook*, 23rd ed., © 1962 by Halley's Bible Handbook Inc., p. 437.

Chapter 4

1. *Parallel Bible Commentary* (Nashville: Thomas Nelson, 1994), Daniel 3:1, P. 1634. The height of Nebuchadnezzar's statue—approximately 90 feet tall.

Chapter 6

1. *New Strong's Exhaustive Concordance of the Bible,* © 1990 by Thomas Nelson Publishers; 1 Samuel 15:23 *witchcraft*; concordance Hebrew word # 7081.

Chapter 8

1. *Parallel Bible Commentary* (Nashville: Thomas Nelson, 1994), "James 1:23-24," p. 2588.

2. Ibid., "James 1:25," p. 2588.

Chapter 9

1. *Halley's Bible Handbook*, 23rd ed., © 1962 by Halley's Bible Handbook, Inc., chap. 37, p. 65

2. Leon Wood, *A Survey of Israel's History*, rev. & enlarged ed. (Grand Rapids: Zondervan, 1986), rev. by David O'Brien, chap. 6, "Life in Egypt," p. 104.

978-0-595-45313-
0-595-45313-9

Printed in the United States
81446LV00003B/208

9 780595 453139